P9-APX-844

THE
iMBiBLE

THE IMBIBLE

Drinking Games for Times You'll Never Remember with Friends You'll Never Forget

Alex Bash

St. Martin's Griffin New York

 Printed in the United States of America. For information, address St. Martin's Press, 175 Fifth Avenue, New York, N.Y. 10010.

www.stmartins.com

Book design by Phil Mazzone

Illustrations by Bryan Berry

Library of Congress Cataloging-in-Publication Data

Bash, Alex.

The imbible : drinking games for times you'll never remember with friends you'll never forget / Alex Bash.—1st ed.

p. cm.

ISBN-13: 978-0-312-38229-2

ISBN-10: 0-312-38229-4

1. Drinking games. 2. Drinking of alcoholic beverages—Humor. I. Title.

GV1202.D74B37 2008

793.2—dc22

2008013011

First Edition: August 2008

10 9 8 7 6 5 4 3 2 1

This book is dedicated to the one truly inspiring icon in my life; an inspiration of heavenly ideals so pure and true; the epitome of what it is to work hard and fight for love and happiness even through the long, hard nights; to the light of my life, the center of my world, and to everything I wish I could be: My Liver.

CONTENTS

After three hours of playing these games your friends, family, co-workers, and most likely your firstborn child, will be drunk. Drunk people are much easier to cheat . . . and draw on with Sharpies . . . and convince to do backflips off the arboretum bridge . . . and use as a dartboard. Thought you should know.

All I can say is, if you decide to play any of these for research, don't lose at Low Man. Unless you are a fridge, in which case, give me a cold one.

Only found in the table of contents!

TOC Drinking Game: Read the table of contents and drink three every time you read the word "drink." Drink, drink, drink, drink, drink, drink, drink, drink. Haha.

Admit it: you've never seen anything like this.

Drink.

INTRODUCTION

Warning/Last Chance to Call and Apologize to Your Girlfriend in Advance for Calling Her a Bitch Later On

BOOZE, BOOZE, BOOZE . . . the social glue that brings together people from all walks of life for the common purpose of making a complete ass of themselves. But rest assured, we're having a really, *really* good time doing it. Yes, our friends may have claimed they didn't know us as we bared our ass to the line of moviegoers from the sunroof of the limousine and, yes, we may have charges pressed against us for public urination and getting the monkeys drunk, but no one—not even our parole officers—can take away the surprisingly forgettable memories we created.

So what exactly do you do when you wake up in an unfamiliar neighborhood, handcuffed to a fire hydrant, clothed in nothing but socks and pink nail polish, your hand clutching a stained legal document . . . written in French? Celebrate! You just had a great night! And to think: it all started with *The Imbible: Drinking Games for Times You'll Never Remember with Friends You'll Never Forget.*

With this book, you'll acquire a vast body of blurry memories full of drunken adventures, hangover remedies, sloshed sexual encounters, and several new cell phones, which you will want to get anyway after your old one tested positive for syphilis. Do not worry, this happens.

From my own hazy recollections of nights long past I have realized twenty key lessons I wish to pass along so you don't wake up at fifty wishing you'd heard a drunken duck quack. It's what midlife crises are made of.

1. Boobs are your friend.
2. You should never attempt to drunkenly surf on top of a car while juggling flaming dildos unless there are at least four cameras rolling or else you'll get peer-pressured into doing it again. Luckily, you won't have that pesky limb to deal with this time.
3. Yes, trees drink the liquid that's in the ground around them; no, you cannot get them drunk; yes, it would be fucking hilarious.
4. No one cares about how much you've drunk except the doctor pumping your stomach.
5. Unless it's a road sign that says Speed Hump, it's not worth stealing.
6. If you ask your friend if he thinks that girl in pink looks like a man but he doesn't hear you and then asks if you think that guy in pink looks like a girl—run.
7. Guys: if you're worried about whiskey dick and don't mind the ensuing spam, you can order Viagra from Canada. Not 100 percent to do with drinking, but worth mentioning.
8. Girls: No one cares about your ex-boyfriend except the psychologist you need to call.
9. You cannot put plastic in the oven. You cannot put plastic in the oven. You cannot put plastic in the oven. You cannot put plastic in the oven.

10. Girls who "forgot" their ID are sixteen. Guys who "forgot" their ID got it suspended after their third DUI.

11. You will never catch a squirrel. Yes, I know it sounds fun, but stick to ducks.

12. Note from my doctor: "Unfortunately, Mr. Bash, drinking from five different cases of beer is not diversifying your diet; you are still missing vodka, rum, whiskey, wine, gin, and a large pizza."

13. Gentlemen: you cannot drink yourself sterile. Now go make those phone calls.

14. If you wake up in a G-string with a bunch of one-dollar bills surrounding your crotch and have no recollection of how it happened, you are awesome. Don't let anybody ever tell you otherwise. Not even the judge.

15. Alcohol is not self-cleaning. I know. I am sorry. I cried, too.

16. If you piss yourself, do not take off your pants and try to dry them helicopter style. Your newly exposed balls will be in serious jeopardy.

17. Drinking faster than your brain can develop a sense of rationality: the best thing since beer-bonging.

18. Contrary to popular belief, you still feel pain while drunk. Oh, and taking an overly ripened orange to the balls from a water-balloon launcher . . . not a good idea.

19. While playing Beer Pong, the amount guys let girls lean over the table is directly proportional to how much cleavage they're showing.

20. Lastly, every awesome memory I have (or have been reminded of) began with a solid night of drinking games.

Drinking games have a long and illustrious history, beginning in the thirteenth century BC, when King Tut realized the people of his nation needed something to break up the monotony of their miserable lives, which had so far been spent growing out their goatees and starving to death. Tut attacked this plague of boredom by imbibing massive quantities of beer and falling out of a window. This fun (but primitive) pastime caught on and soon became popular with the masses.

Shortly thereafter, the practice of drunken debauchery was improved upon by the creation of less painful drinking games, such as Thumper!, Beer Pong, and Flip Cup, often looked upon as defining moments in the history of Western civilization. During the Middle Ages, the perfection of such games served as indisputable evidence for the existence of God.

Drinking games have been right there with us ever since:

- William Shakespeare played so much Beer Die that all he could write were made-up words in his own nonsense language.
- Although the evidence was suppressed by the Warren Commission, highly placed sources within the Central Intelligence Agency will one day reveal that the assassination of President John F. Kennedy was the direct result of a game of Asshole gone terribly, terribly wrong.
- Scholars now believe the fall of the Soviet Union was not due to the collapse of the Russian economy but to the infamous game of Quarters that took place at the 1986 Reykjavik Summit between Mikhail Gorbachev and Ronald Reagan.

Not only have drinking games shaped the past, but I also have evidence that they can help us stay healthy, rich, and happy. Several scientific studies that I unfortunately forgot to cite have also bolstered the need to play more drinking games:

- In a number of controlled studies, scientists wearing long white coats and thick glasses determined that if we drink one liter of water a day for a year, we will ingest one kilo of *Escherichia coli,* known to the scientific community as "poop." Lesson: It's better to drink turd-free beer and act stupid than to drink water and be full of shit.

- Numerous studies done by old white men with acronyms after their names concluded that people who drink alcohol earn 10 to 14 percent more annually because they're out networking, occasionally sleeping with their boss, and robbing banks when blacked out. Cheers to an early retirement! (No but, seriously, they do earn more.)
- Another study conducted by my friend's wealthy stepdad showed that playing drinking games with your wife and seeing who can sign his or her name faster on the ~~prenuptial agreement~~ unimportant random piece of paper can make you a lot ~~richer~~ happier.
- One final study conducted by myself observed how much fun people had when they played drinking games versus when they poked themselves in the eye repeatedly with a crude gardening implement. My results don't lie: drinking games are exceptionally fun—hell, even my newly blind friends enjoy them!

Despite those excellent bullet points, some people despise alcohol because they feel trapped by alcoholism. I, on the other hand, am trapped by realityism. Answer me this: does being drunk suck? No. Does reality suck? Sometimes. So now we have this: drunk=not sucking, reality=kind of sucking. This is the same difference between a million dollars and a leech: a million dollars does not suck, a leech does. So what's it gonna be, riches or leeches? I've made my point.

Then there are people who think drinking alcohol is bad for you. This could not be further from the truth. They say it hurts your liver. Well, let me ask them this: How do you get stronger muscles? By working them out, then letting them rest. This is why we work our liver six days a week, then let it recover on Wednesday. Our livers could kick their liver's ass!

These health freaks also must not have heard how good red wine is for the heart because I still see them running on treadmills—suckers! As soon as this book falls into the hands of the surgeon general, expect the cardio side of the gym to be lined with wine tastings and, instead of water fountains, there'll be barrels of wine! Just place your cup under the tap, and *bam!* heart-saving French Burgundy spills out. Scared that you'll drop a dumbbell on yourself after too much heart-juice? Just stop using weights, too! See, the heart pumps blood through your entire body, *including* your muscles, so the healthier your heart gets, the more blood it will pump through your muscles, which is the whole point of using free weights in the first place, right? Instead of spending thirty minutes a day pounding out *reps,* spend that time pounding back *red.*

If you're not out there strengthening your heart and liver just yet, then I have one last bit of advice to share, which I received from a certified personal trainer (seriously): "To really tone your muscles, you need to work those little 'stabilizer' muscles that large movements and classic lifts don't work."

This used to be an experts-only piece of information, but new studies show that the body works the stabilizer muscles best when done naturally, so they suggest that at least three times a week you walk to a bar, drink yourself into a state of intoxication rivaling a coma, and then stumble your way home. He continued . . . "The amount of balance you'll need to make it home will be more than enough to work even the tiniest of stabilizer muscles, and the hour you spend trying to call your ex-girlfriend will keep your fingers nice and nimble."

At least that's how I heard it.

Reading this book and heeding its advice can also take the place of meditation and spirituality. When you drink, your mind relaxes itself and many subconscious thoughts you don't even realize are there come to the front of your mind. These sublevel feelings may be the sudden desire to get naked and act out "I'm a Little Teapot," declare your love for an inanimate object, fight your neighbor's prized roses, or even cry from your repressed anger over the season finale of *Grey's Anatomy.* Sometimes you even speak your own language that no one else can understand—try doing that in some Tibetan temple! Ha!

Not only do you get in touch with yourself while drunk, but you get in touch with the world around you. Usually you don't even notice how hard the earth is working to stay in orbit, but after a three-hour Chumbawumba marathon, you can really feel the force of the world spinning at 66,600 miles an hour as you continually fall over (who could stay balanced at that speed!?). Ever kissed the grass while sober? How about hugged a bush? I can honestly say the only time my lips have purposely come in contact with Father Earth was while intoxicated; we've been closer ever since.

If you start to use this book more often than you think you should, relax—you're not an alcoholic; you just enjoy imbibing large amounts of alcohol on a frequent basis to further your enjoyment of daily activities. Also, you don't go to meetings to talk about booze, unless you choose "beer brands" for the "categories" card drawn in Kings.

Please, for the sake of increasing the world's good times per capita, take a gander at my favorite drinking games and turn your night of crying and masturbation into an alcohol-soaked receipt from the San Diego Zoo, Beer Pong with the mayor's daughter, and an expensive bar tab covered in phone numbers you will never call.

So locate your pants, polish off that twelve-pack, and prepare to embark on a journey you will most likely never tell your spouse.

Oh, and before we begin, I have a few things to say . . .

1. Although explaining jokes and clever comments relieves them of their humor, I get asked so often that I really must: *imbibe* means "to drink." Thus, this book is the bible (set of rules) for imbibing (drinking). It's clever. Shut up.

2. When a game refers to a "drink," as in "drink three for being a moron," it does not mean you must drink three beers. A drink is basically a gulp, but be sure to adjust this for what you're drinking. For example, if you're drinking Bud Light and you have to drink fifteen, drink all of them; it'll be, like, one beer. But if you're shooting straight rum like a champ bound for cirrhosis, then I wouldn't recommend it. However, if someone chooses to waive my expert advice, get the Sharpies ready and practice drawing genitalia on an uneven surface.

3. When explaining games, I will almost always use *he, his,* and *him.* I'm not sexist, but typing *he or she* or *his or her* all the time is really fucking annoying. That, and I really don't care.

4. I am not responsible for any pain or trouble you get yourself into. If you get an MIP, DUI, arrested, injured, herpes, married to your favorite sofa cushion, or do anything involving an illegally imported Komodo dragon, I am not sorry, but you should e-mail me to party if you're ever in Seattle. (Seriously: alexbash1@gmail.com.)

5. Lastly, if you are not of legal drinking age, you should try to not get caught drinking alcohol, be an incredibly fast runner, or have a really kick-ass fake ID.

CLASSIC GAMES!

BEER PONG

Origin: Babylon, 2300 BC

Creator: God (eleventh commandment: Thou shalt not break plane of table with elbow).

Story: Originally played vertically in the Hanging Gardens; the Babylonians would use L-shaped cups to hold the beer and throw crude rocks instead of Ping-Pong balls, because Ping-Pong balls were for "Persian wusses." (Note: Far from being wusses, the Persians eventually conquered Babylon and covered it in overpriced rugs. They then pissed in their gardens whenever drunk, which proved difficult as they were in "hanging" gardens and it often ended with someone getting pee in their face. This was the precursor for the drunken prank "golden shower.")

Players: Two teams of one to five people each. Works best with two teams of two. If there are more players, just add one Ping-Pong ball for each two new members (one on each side); and six cups and two beers per new player. And a kick to the crotch for making things difficult. They'll drink themselves numb soon, anyway.

Supplies:

- Six keg cups for each player on either team
- One table ten to twenty feet long and wide enough to hold all the keg cups

- Two Ping-Pong balls. (Or, two crude rocks if you're Babylonian.)
- A mouth to talk unjustified shit to opponents. (Very crucial.)

Beer: Two beers for every six cups, distributed as evenly as your drunken sense of proportion will allow. No, that's not an overflowing cup, Drunk Steve. It's the dog, and you can't drink him.

Objective: Throw your Ping-Pong ball into the cups arranged artfully in pyramids in front of your opponents. If you make the ball in the cup, you must make a sexual joke regarding the entrance of the ball(s) into the cup's hole, and then your opponent must drink the beer from the cup the ball landed in. If he fails to first remove the ball, you can either (a) help out the gene pool by letting him choke on the beer-soaked Ping-Pong ball and thankfully never reproduce, or (b) steal his beer while he's choking and hand it out to girls; both are acceptable by Beer Pong doctrine. The sunken ball is then returned to you so you can add still more humiliation to your pathetic opponent's life. When all of a team's cups are gone, its members lose . . . and they're drunk! Hooray!

Setup and Gameplay: The game begins with each player lining up his six keg cups in the form of a triangle (3-2-1, with the triangle pointing toward his opponents) and pouring two beers evenly among the cups. The cups must all be touching. However, if the beer-covered table floats a cup away, leave it be—the beer has spoken.

Each team starts with one ball (if there are more than two per side, just work it out evenly). Players stand next to their teammates, across the table from their opponents. Do I really need to tell you the table should be positioned lengthwise?

If a ball is thrown and not made, it's anybody's ball. There are no turns in Beer Pong! The only exceptions are if (a) somebody is injured (e.g., twisted ankle, gunshot wound, PABS [Pussy-Ass Bitch Syndrome]) and therefore can't properly fight for the ball,

(b) there's way too much stuff crowding the room (tables, chairs, bodies), or (c) you're a wuss.

Very important: When you throw the ball, imagine there is an invisible plane going up at the edge of the table. No part of your body, arm, or hand can break this plane. You cannot lean over the table and throw the ball. You must stand back and throw from behind the edge of the table. If you violate this rule, your opponents can laugh at you mercilessly.

If both balls are thrown by the same team and land in the same cup, that counts as three cups. The team that threw the balls chooses which three cups the other team drinks. (Note: This rarely happens; balls are usually flying everywhere and nobody is throwing at the same time.)

If a ball is *bounced* by a team and goes into a cup, it counts as two cups. But if a ball is bounced, it can be swatted by the other team after the first bounce. This strategy is often used when the other team is not paying attention. It is also very effective when you're playing against people who have no hand-eye coordination. Or are blind. And deaf.

If a player interferes with a thrown ball before it hits a cup or the table, that player must remove one cup from his side as a penalty. (And drink its contents, obviously. This isn't a "removing" game, it's a drinking game.)

When a ball lands in a cup, the beer in that cup must be drunk immediately, *before* the player is allowed to set it down.

This is motivation to drink faster, as it's hard to fight for a ball with one hand holding a beer. If a player violates this rule, he must drink another cup as well, forcing the player to double-fist, thus making it easier to bounce against him, fight for balls, and whack him in the nuts with an inflatable prostitute doll.

Each team gets one "rerack" per game, meaning after they've made, say, eight of their opponents' twelve cups and the remaining four are all spread out, they can have them combined into a diamond.

If you are scared of germs, you can have a cup of water next to your pyramid and cleanse the ball after it has touched the floor, landed in a cup, or been in the hands of that sweaty gross dude who smells like rancid milk from your Chem 126 lab—unless you're into that kind of thing.

If one of your cups gets knocked over by a Ping-Pong ball or by a teammate's hand/arm while trying to protect it or going for balls, that cup is gone, you are one cup closer to losing, and you have wasted beer. I hope you don't need to be told what a disaster this is. So make sure you fill each cup enough. If they are almost empty, they'll get knocked over real quick.

Options: The following are various "house rules" I have stumbled across in my life of Pong; some made me appreciate the game a little more, others found me on the roof of the restaurant I worked at, taking tequila shots with my boss at four A.M. It's up to you whether these rules (or their outcome) are a good thing.

- When you begin the game, one player from each team gets a Pong, looks his opponent in the eye, and shoots without breaking the stare. Whoever makes it first gets to start the game with both balls. Kind of odd, but some people do it ritualistically (Note: This is a great time to wear sunglasses or a push-up bra).
- You always take turns throwing as teams, and only get the balls back if you make both of them on the same turn (since this

rarely happens, I suggest one of you pelt your opponents in the face while the other bounces).

- Most of the time when the last cup is gone, the game is over. Lately, though, I've noticed that people like the "rebuttal shot": if your last cup gets sunk, each player on your team has one last chance to shoot but has to make all of the other team's cups to stay alive. Good for people who work well under pressure, like contract killers (Note: The government has spies who monitor your rebuttal-shot average; 66 percent or more and they can off you without explanation).
- The wild'n'wacky'n'crazy'n'wacky'n'wild setup rule! Each team can set up its cups however the hell it wants: instead of a triangle, you can do a straight line, two squares, or spell out "fuck you" or "munch on my chode" or "you will most likely not win this match, but I wish you the best of luck." You may need extra cups.
- Some people are quite adamant about removing a cup after it is sunk. Generally, if you're playing with turns, don't remove it and give each other a chance to make both Pongs in one; but if you're playing free-for-all, then remove the cup before it gets sunk (if you even notice it)!
- This one friend I have has this rule that says no attractive female can wear clothing. His name is Me.

Strategy:

- Each player, if there are two of you, should cover one side of dthe table for loose balls, as opposed to both going for that one loose ball (because your opponent could then *bounce* the other ball in). If there are three of you, have the two outside people go after balls off the table and the middle person catch balls on the table, block bounces, and remove cups that have been sunk before a second ball lands in them.
- If you can control yourself while playing free-for-all, try to get all the balls on your side for each throw so you can (a) make

them both into the same cup if possible, (b) have one person throw while the other bounces, or (c) throw all the balls at once, thus confusing your opponents and gaining a better chance at getting one of the loose balls. Or, my personal favorite, pelt two balls at their faces and bounce the other. This could get dirty, especially if you replace the Ping-Pong balls with clumps of dirt.

- But remember—Beer Pong is only a game. That is, unless that blond chick from Kappas is watching, and that dick from Sigma Nu is your opponent, and you have to be at the Quad in fifteen minutes dressed as one of the Village People for the Box Car Derby Race. Emotions can definitely run high, so it's in your best interest to drink yourself numb.

FLIP CUP

Operation Imbibe & Conquer: Instead of dropping bombs during wars, we should send over massive quantities of beer, 3 million copies of this book, and pictures of Scarlett Johansson. As soon as they reach the drunken sing-along stage of intoxication we can parachute in, install democracy, and recycle the cans for war reparations. Contributions for the 2012 presidential campaign are always welcome.

Players: As many people as you can put along the length of your table. Teams must have the same number of participants. If one team has Blacked-Out Bill, maybe put two on the other to compensate. As for No-Hands Ned . . . sorry, bud—go sit in the corner. No one likes a disabled drinker.

Supplies:

- A flat table
- One keg cup per person—two if you're badass

Beer: Enough to make onlookers think you're Keystone Light marketing reps

Mythical Creature of Flip Cup: The hydra (also a good team name)

Objective: Be the first team to flip all your cups over and tell the other team how much better you are at life

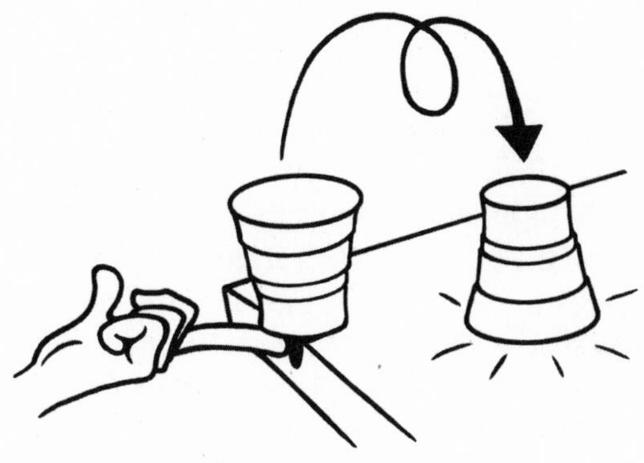

Basics: Teams line up on either side of the table with their cups in front of them, filled one-third of the way with delicious beer.

Pick an end of the table to be the starting end; the two players facing each other start the game.

Everybody counts down together from three to zero to make sure all are paying attention. At zero, the two starters cheer with their cups, touch them to the table, and then chug them down as fast as possible. When the starters finish, they quickly set their respective cup upright on the table halfway over the edge, and tip the part hanging off with their fingers just enough to make the cup flip over onto the table and land upside down. It doesn't matter if the cup flips a half-rotation or ten; if it lands upside down, it counts.

If the cup doesn't sit upside down, the starter must grab it (hurry!) and try again. Each player keeps going until he gets the cup to land and stay upside down on the table, then the next person in line on that team goes. The first team to get all its cups flipped wins. Initiate chest bumps and belittling of opponents.

Strategy:

- Gentlemen, nobody knows why, but ladies *love* the Flip Cup.
- As far as flipping technique? Put your cup down and . . . flip it. If it doesn't land upside down, flip it again. That's okay. We'll wait.
- A more difficult way to play this is to set the cups on the edge of the table already upside down and flip them right side up, because the upright position has a smaller surface area on which to land and balance (it's science). Also, people's shoes get covered in beer if they don't finish their whole cup. Cheaters.
- Guys, be a man and always fill your cup up at least one-third of the way, if not more. Ladies, same thing. No sympathy.

Options/Other Shit:

- For those wishing to maximize drunkenness, the game can be structured so that each team goes down *and* back. To do this, the last player on each side (a.k.a. the Corner Man) has to have two cups and get them both flipped before his team can start heading back to the front of the line. The Corner Man is usually the best Flip Cup player, or at least the one who is the least drunk. Also, everybody else has to have beer ready to refill his cup after he successfully lands his first one, so he has a cup to drink and flip on the way back.

- If you're really trying to get loaded quickly, you can pour a shot of hard alcohol instead of beer into each cup and not let the drinker have the chaser until he's flipped his cup successfully.

- The isn't called Grab Cup or Hold Cup, so there is, of course, no holding onto the cup in any way as you flip it over. You can only touch the bottom of the cup, and only for an instant, as if spanking its cute little plastic butt.

- There is also, of course, no interfering with the other team's cups in any way. If an accidental cup collision occurs, don't worry about it. Neither of your cups probably landed, anyway.

- If you think you're something special, try flipping the cup over with your hand behind your back, under your leg, with your tongue, or by flexing your erection. No, seriously.

For the Extremist: Just as Extreme Ironers took pressing clothes to the next level, groups of Extreme Flip Cuppers are willing to risk as much as momentary embarrassment to make the Flip Cup record books. There are legends of games that stretched across an entire football field. Some believers say that two brave men played with five-gallon buckets in the place of cups, their failed livers having to be buried miles underground to save Earth from the toxicity. If you think you have the guts and lack of regard for your physical well-being to make Flip Cup history, please, send the pictures to me at alexbash1@gmail.com along with the obit, so I can pay tribute.

HIGH, LOW, RED, BLACK

How This Game May Have Been Created: The differing limitations involved in simultaneous measurements of subatomic particles had dire implications for our choice to consciously combine the electromagnetic photons via nucleon-fibrosis due to the diffraction of the oscillation field. Thus, electrolysis conducted the osmosis of the protons' rapidly crystallizing from the outer ring of alkalinity of the appropriated doctrine of desalinization.

How This Game Was Actually Created: A bunch of dudes playing cards wanted to do something fun to get drunk and make penis jokes.

Players: Two or more

Supplies: A deck of cards

Beer: More than you previously thought you could consume

Miscellaneous Conversation:

Toilet: Hey, how's it going man?
Dude: Blllaaahhhhh!!
Toilet: Did you see that new brunette?
Dude: Blllaaahhhhh!!
Toilet: So how about those Mariners?
Dude: Well, I believe that with some solid off-season trades, call-ups from the minors, and a reliable first-round draft pick, we could really be in contention for that pennant.
Toilet: And how's school going?
Dude: Bllllaaaahhhh!!

Objective: To correctly guess five times in a row if the next card turned over will be higher or lower than the previous card or, at the player's choice, if it will be red or black. Or green, if there's LSD involved.

Counting Cards: One person plays at a time while the rest egg him on to mess up so he drinks himself retarded. Anyone can be the dealer. Play starts when the dealer lays down one card.

Whoever is up guesses whether the next card turned over from the top of the deck will be higher than the previous card, lower than the previous card, or red or black.

He only gets one guess, and then the next card is laid down next to the first one. If he is correct, he keeps going until he either guesses incorrectly or correctly guesses five cards in a row.

If he correctly guesses five in a row, he does not have to drink; the turn moves on to the next person and the previous player's five correctly guessed cards are shuffled back into the deck. If he guesses incorrectly, he drinks one drink for each card on the table, not counting the first card laid down by the dealer at the beginning.

When somebody guesses incorrectly, it's the next player's turn. The game moves clockwise (to the left, you digitized idiot).

Strategy: Didn't you watch *Rounders*? If it's a low card, guess high. If it's a high card, guess low. If it's a medium card, guess red or black. It doesn't matter. Even when you lose, you win—because you're getting drunk!

[Variation 1:] A slightly more harsh/awesome way to play the game: if Player One guesses five cards correctly, Player Two is up like normal, but you do not remove the five cards already on the table that Player One guessed correctly. Player Two simply continues on guessing off Player One's last card, adding Player One's cards to his stack. So, if Player One guesses all five cards right, and then Player Two guesses his first card incorrectly, he drinks six. If

Players One, Two, and Three all guess five cards in a row correctly (fifteen total) and then Player Four incorrectly guesses his first card, he drinks sixteen. This game can get very brutal if you are good guessers. Do not play this game with Miss Cleo or anyone else with verifiable psychic powers.

[Variation 2:] If a card is laid down and it's the same one as the card directly behind it, the current guesser drinks double. For example, let's say there are ten cards on the table, the last one being the eight of diamonds. Bob says the next card will be lower than an eight. The next card is the eight of spades. Bob drinks twenty-two (the eleven cards showing, times two). Good night, Bob!

[Variation 3:] One player *must* continue guessing and drinking until he gets five cards correctly in a row. So, if Player One incorrectly guesses his third card, he drinks three and starts over at the first card, and keeps guessing and drinking until he correctly guesses five in a row. This can make his drink count stack up higher than empty pizza boxes on a fraternity house floor. The unintentional record for drinks in one turn is approximately one hundred. To make the game move faster, it is okay to "owe" the drinks you've accumulated instead of drink all of them when you finally guess five in a row.

[Variation 4:] Utilize Variation 2. Go to a random park. Get a trick deck of all aces. See who can find his way home first after waking up from his blackout (each article of clothing lost adds a five-minute penalty to your time. Each bra acquired subtracts three).

BASEBALL

History of Baseball: In 1845, Alexander Cartwright of New York State invented a uniquely American pastime based on the English game of Rounders. Cartwright and his New York Knickerbockers Baseball Club devised the first rules and regulations of the modern game of baseball, to maximize beer consumption among spectators.

At some point after that, a bunch of fraternity guys with too many quarters and too much time on their hands found a way to adapt the rules of baseball into an indoor game intended to get people much drunker than they could ever be at a real game, except, maybe, in the bleachers at Fenway Park.

Players: An even number of teams, each comprised of one to three players

Supplies:

- Four shot glasses
- A couple of quarters. You only need one at a time, but you'll probably lose a few in the eighth or ninth inning after someone nails his fourteenth grand slam.
- A flat table
- Paper and something to write with, and then more paper after the first sheet gets covered in beer

Beer: What your grandmother would call "a disgusting amount"

Objective: To score more runs than the other team before the ninth inning is over and not wake up with a Yankees tattoo on your left butt cheek

Play Ball! The "away" team is up to bat first, just like in real baseball. The away team is the team that either doesn't live at the place where you're playing or, if they do, they live the farthest away from the table at which you're playing. You start by setting up the four shot glasses in a straight line going away from you (the first glass is closest to you, the fourth is farthest away). Fill up the shot glasses with beer, wine, or a mixed drink. Not hard alcohol shots, unless you *want* your stomach pumped. (Note: Getting one's stomach pumped not a weight-loss technique.)

Each player takes turns bouncing the quarter to try to get it into the shot glasses. The first and closest shot glass is a single, the second a double, the third a triple, and the fourth is a home run. When the player who is "up at bat" sinks the quarter, *he* drinks, not the opposite team, and then refills. If you hit a single, you drink only the single glass. If you hit a double, drink both the double glass and the single glass. If you hit a triple, you drink the triple, double, and single glasses; and if you hit a home run, you drink all four. This is one of those games in which you're rewarded for your performance. The better you do, the drunker you get. It also helps even out the playing field if one team sucks at bouncing quarters and the other team rocks your nipples off (see illustration on how to properly bounce a quarter).

If you make it into a cup, your imaginary runners advance around the bases. Runs are scored in the same way as in real baseball, which I am not going to explain—if you don't know them, come out from under your rock and ask somebody. Whenever you don't make the quarter into one of the shot glasses, it counts as an out. There are three outs for each team, each inning. When a team gets three outs, its players finish whatever was left in their shot glasses and give the glasses to the other team so they can fill them up with their drinks. Use paper and something to write with to keep track of the score, where runners are on base, how many outs there are, and what inning it is. This is very easy to forget, especially when you're drunk and telling exaggerated stories of your high school baseball career ("I swear to God, man—naked chicks in the dugout!").

Sharpening your Cleats:

- It's fun to give yourself the name of a famous baseball player and use that name every time you play. Or, if you're a major fan, name your team after a real one and go through the batting order. It will be just like real baseball, except you probably won't be taking as many steroids.
- If you have no life, you can keep track of all your stats (hits, home runs, win-loss record, puke-and-rallies, etc.) throughout the "season," which could be as long as a week, a semester at school, or a full calendar year. At the end of the year, give out awards: MVP, Rookie of the Year, Most Likely to Miss the Playoffs Because of a Stint in Rehab, and so on.
- Instead of shot glasses, try using four cups, each one taller than the next. The shortest of the cups is a single and the tallest a home run.
- Real games last for nine innings, with each team up at bat once per inning. This can prove to be entirely too long for players of a low drinking tolerance, especially if they're good. Before the game, decide how many innings you're going to play, so there's no bickering later on if someone wants to tap out. The beautiful thing is, if you're doing really well and scoring lots of runs, you'll get so drunk that you'll start missing the shot glasses and not drink anymore. It's perfect!
- Don't be that guy who names himself Mike Oxbig. I mean, come on now—we all went streaking together. You're not fooling anyone.

Bouncing a Quarter:

The best way to bounce a quarter for maximum distance and height while still maintaining accuracy is to hold it by the edges between your thumb and index finger so the face on the quarter is visible and facing you. Try to keep the quarter perfectly flat and hit it down onto the table so as much of the quarter hits the table as possible. Try to make it hit the table two to three inches in front of the glass you're trying to make it into. The harder you slam it down, the higher you go. Hey—just like drinking!

KINGS

Story Time: Once upon a time, a group of crows decided to play Kings. It was going well until that fucker Joey pulled a nine of clubs and everybody had to rhyme. The game never ended because all Joey could say was "Caw!" which of course rhymed quite well with Dwayne's "Caw!" which sounded just like Ernie's "Caw!" Rumor has it you can still hear crows playing this same game even today, flying around yelling "Caw!"

Caution: Kings not recommended for birds.

Players: Three or more. The more the merrier, and the drunker! Hooray!

Supplies: A fifty-two-card deck and one large cup on which to balance the cards. Or, just open the passed-out guy's mouth and lay the cards on top. If cards move due to breathing, use tape.

Beer: Various kinds of beer. Or vodka. Or wine. Or rum, gin, whiskey, spiked punch, schnapps, an alcoholic's blood sample, the sweat of a rock star, and so on.

Official Sport of Kings: Cricket. Although I think Kings has been sleeping with Ice Skating (*way* nicer tits).

Objective: There are no winners. Everybody just keeps drawing and drinking until the fourth king is drawn. You then apologize to the community for the illegible vandalism and fifteen choruses of "Wonder Wall" at 3: 30 A.M. Also, the Louis and Clark Memorial "was like that when you got there" (Note: Louis and Clark Memorial not like that when you got there; doggie style not yet invented).

Cracking the Crown: The game begins by spreading the cards out face down in a circle around the cup. Player One draws a card at random from the circle; each card has a different rule associated with it. These rules are highly disputed and frequently argued over, but I am here to put a stop to it. These are the official rules of Kings; however, there is an entirely different way to play the game that is slightly more crude and daring and awesome, and comes next as Kings II.

If the card you draw is a . . .

2: It's for you. Choose somebody to drink one.

3: It's for me. Drink one.

4: It's for the floor. Last person to touch his head to the surface on which the cards lay drinks two. It is called "for the floor" because Kings was originally played by the Old Testament's now-famous Three Kings on their way to see Jesus. Watch as heads go slamming to the table—hilarious.

5: It's for guys. Whoever has a penis consumes one.

6: It's for chicks. Whoever does not have a penis consumes one.

7: Play Reach for Heaven. Last person to raise his drink to the sky drinks one. Watch as beer goes flying everywhere (white shirts on females recommended).

8: Play Pick a Date. Choose somebody: this person has to drink whenever you drink for the next ten turns, and vice versa.

9: Play Bust a Rhyme. You say a one-liner, ending with whatever word you want. You *can't* just say one word, like *bar*. The next person has to say a line—as if rapping—that also rhymes with the first player's line. Whoever doesn't rhyme or takes too long drinks two.

Rhyme example:

Player One: "My name is Steve and I'm so fine."
Player Two: "Steve takes it in the ass all the time."
Player Three: "Steve can't even hold down wine."
Crow: "Caw!"
Everybody: "Drink, Crow!" (Crow is drinking because *Caw* doesn't rhyme with *wine* and is only one word. Crow would drink for either of these reasons.)

10: Make a rule. Everybody *must* follow your rule. Popular examples follow.

J: Play Categories. The card drawer names a category, such as car companies, beer makers, sex positions, fallen communist leaders, etc., and each person after him must name something in that category without repeating or taking too long. This keeps going around the circle until someone messes up, at which time five drinks are rewarded.

Q: Play Questions. Look at someone and ask him a question. Players then go around asking one another questions in no particular order, except that you can't ask a question of the person who just asked you. Whoever answers or says anything other than a question drinks two and is made fun of.

Example of "questions:"

Spot: "How's it going, Robi?"
Robi: "Why is he asking me?" (looking at TheHamster)
TheHamster: "How are those herpes treating you?" (looking at Sarah)

Sarah: "Do I even know you?" (looking at JV)
JV: "Yeah, we robbed that liquor store yesterday."
Everyone: "Drink, JV!" (JV is drinking because he didn't ask a question, and because he is a complete moron.)

K: Play King's Cup. Pour as much as you want of your drink into the center cup. This could be beer, gin and tonic, vodka, or whatever else you happen to be drinking. Place the king on the rim of the cup. Whoever draws the fourth king drinks whatever is in the cup, the game ends, and you show him where the toilet is to puke.

A: Play Waterfall. The card drawer starts drinking, and everyone else starts drinking with him. No one can stop drinking until the person on his right stops. So, Player One, the drawer, would start drinking and everyone would follow suit. Only when he stops can Player Two stop, and only when Player Two stops can Player Three stop, and so on. Basically the last person gets screwed.

Stratagy:

- The game moves clockwise.
- Make sure everybody playing knows the rules and what they mean before you start, so you aren't all hammered and trying to explain what "Questions" is. Or just never explain and make them drink. Damn uneducated drunks . . .

Some popular rules to make up when you draw a ten are:

The Thumb Master/Row Master/Head Master: You are the Thumb Master, and whenever you put your thumb so casually on the table, everybody else has to follow suit and the last person to do so drinks how ever much you decided when making the rule. Same thing with Row Master; begin to subtly row your imaginary canoe and the last one to follow drinks. Head Master is fucking hilarious: place your head on the table (not too hard!)

and watch as everybody scrambles to slam his head down to the table.

The words drink, drank, and drunk cannot be said: Each is punishable by one drink. Or death. Whatever you like.

No real names: Give everybody a nickname based on something embarrassing about the person or something stupid that he did while blacked out. Like hook up with Shamu (sorry, Shane). Any saying of a real name results in one drink.

You you have have to to say say every every word word twice twice: Or or else else you you drink drink three three.

You may also use your ten to repeal a rule: You might do this if you become annoyed by the fact that you had to drink three because, when you slammed your head to the table, you only said, "Ouch," once.

KINGS II

Let Us Begin with a Lesson: Boobs are patient. Boobs are kind. Boobs do not get angry if you don't take them out to dinner. Boobs are always content with just being boobs. Sometimes boobs like to be squeezed. Sometimes boobs like to play in the sun. Boobs can take the place of a pillow. Boobs can file your taxes for you. Boobs always know who won the game. Boobs don't ask if you are drinking, they get you a drink. You can take boobs to the movies. Boobs can play football with you. If you misspell *boob,* you get Bob, and Bob is a cool guy. Boobs are perfect for whipped cream tequila shots. Boobs are patient. Boobs are kind. Boobs are good.

Players: Three or more people who don't get upset about degrading themselves

Supplies: A fifty-two-card deck, one cup

Beer: A drink that gets you drunk

Kings II's Favorite Quote: Kings II is currently on trial for assault charges and is unavailable to comment.

Objective: Everybody just keeps drawing cards until the fourth king is drawn. The winner is the first one to pass out. The prize is one less eyebrow to have to deal with.

Staging a Mutiny: The game begins by spreading the cards out face down in a circle around the cup. The first person draws a card at random from the circle; each card has a different rule associated with it. These rules are sometimes argued over, but seeing as I am the ultimate rule master, you will do whatever I say. And get me a Coke. These are the slightly more crude and daring rules. The official rules for regular Kings are listed one game back on pages 21–30.

If the card you draw is a . . .

- **2:** It's for "social!" Everybody drinks three.
- **3:** It's for "balls!" and is confusing. So, the card drawer says, "One." Then, going clockwise, each person says the next number (two, three, four, five . . .). However, if the number is a multiple of seven or eleven, or has a seven in it such as thirty-seven, the person must yell, "Balls!" instead of the number, and then the circle changes direction. For example, the first person says, "One," the second says, "Two," and so on: 3, 4, 5, 6, balls! 8, 9, 10, balls! 12, 13, balls! 15, 16, balls! 18, 19, 20, balls! balls! 23, 24, etc. Whenever someone messes up, he drinks five. Keep going until, as a group, you get to fifty without messing up, or at least pretending you didn't.
- **4:** It's for whores. Bitches, consume.
- **5:** It's for "fuck." When this card is turned over, everyone must yell "Fuck!" Last one to do so drinks five.

6: It's for dicks. Dudes, lets make some bad decisions.

7: It's for blow jobs. Yes, blow jobs. The drawer needs to inform the group of either (a) how many people have given him blow jobs (for guys), or (b) how many guys she has given blow jobs to (for girls). However, he or she can choose to say either the truth or a lie, and it's up to the rest of the group to determine which it is. If the group is right the drawer drinks five, if the drawer fools them they each drink three.

8: Play Hate. Pick someone to start drinking; tell him when to start and also when to stop. However, if he finishes his drink before you say, "Stop," you have to finish yours. Here's the catch: your eyes must be closed.

9: Play Dare. You dare somebody to do something crazy, and if he doesn't, he drinks ten. Go wild with this one.

10: It's for text messaging. The player who draws this card must give his cell phone to the rest of the players, who get to send one text message to anyone they want in that person's phone book. Bosses, clients, and current partners are off limits, but ex-girlfriends, parents, or someone the player is trying to hook up with is always good for laughter and worry. If the player doesn't have a cell phone, he drinks five and everybody gets to make "Where have you been for the last decade?" jokes.

J: It's for sexual innuendo. The card drawer picks a category, such as golf. Everybody goes around in a circle making sexual innuendos, such as, "I've got a twelve-inch three wood back at my place you should come try out." Keep going until someone either can't think of one, takes too long, or his innuendo blows, such as, "Baby, I could drive your clit three hundred yards." And then seek mental help, you sick fuck.

Q: Play Ass on the Object. Don't question it. Before the game starts, as a group you choose an object (the neighbor's front door, a bedpost, somebody's face) and, whenever a queen is drawn, everybody races to put their naked ass on that object. Last one drinks four. If you easily get uncomfortable, the wall is a good choice because nobody's ass will come close to yours. If you have butt herpes . . . well, that must suck.

K: Play King's Cup. If you draw a king, pour however much of your drink you want into the center cup; it doesn't matter what your drink is (vodka, gin, beer, etc.). Whoever draws the fourth king drinks it down. If he pukes or can't finish it, he drinks a full cup of whatever he has.

A: Play Insults. Each player goes in a circle insulting the person next to him, but can't use any real curse words (shit, fuck, damn, cunt, dick, chode-muncher, lawyer, New York Met, etc.). Think insults used by fourth graders or your little brother. First one to cuss, repeat, or take too long drinks three.

Other Rules about the Rules:

- The game moves clockwise.
- Explain the rules beforehand so you aren't all hammered while trying to explain what "Balls!" is.

Quick Reminder About Boobs: Boobs, in every respect, are good for mankind. They bring nourishment to babies, attention to emotionally unstable women, and boners to preadolescent boys. However, since we all know the mind of a drunken male is roughly that of a twelve-year-old, he is naturally drawn to the breast region of the female figure, delighting in its warm squishiness. Females, on the other hand, need a way to control these drunken boys, and boobies are just the way to do it. No need to read up on the forty-eight laws of power or increase your knowledge of the local football team, just push up those oddly attractive lumps of fatty tissue and come drink our beer!

SPOONS

Why Do We Play Spoons? Spoons, as we all know, are in second place to forks in the "2008 Utensil Importance Cup." This is a problem because forks, as you also know, are communists. If forks win the Cup, the entire utensil world will be turned upside down. Placings in the Cup are judged by usage of the utensil, so the more we all use spoons, the better the chance they have of being the most important utensil in 2008! The drinking game Spoons is a great way to help out, so do your part and save the utensil world from those damn communist forks!

Players: Three to thirteen. If you have more than thirteen players, you'll run out of cards. And get chlamydia.

Supplies:

- One spoon for each player . . . minus one (if five people are playing, get four spoons)
- A fifty-two-card deck of cards
- A round table. King Arthur style, baby.

Beer: If you're not good with cards, a case should do. If you are good with cards, a case should do.

Spoons—A Metaphor for Life: We love spoons because they're curvy, and curves are good, useful, and well rounded: just like life should be. A knife is too straight and mundane, and a fork is too spread out and undecidedly lost among three or four lifestyles. So be like a spoon and create some curves in your own life, possibly by using a spoon to get those last few ounces of spiked punch into your drink.

Objective: To keep passing cards around until you get four of a kind, and then grab a spoon before anyone else does. Don't be left without a spoon!

Basics of Spooning: Everybody sits around a table within arm's reach of the people on either side. Set the spoons in the very middle of the table, close enough so that everybody can reach one. Do not face any of them toward anybody in particular, because one person would not have one facing him, as you should have one less spoon than there are players. Everybody takes turns being the dealer because he will decide the speed of the game as well as the number of drinks the loser and the semilosers will drink, which he must decide *before* the game begins (I'll explain "semiloser" later). The dealer passes out four cards to each player including himself and sets the deck just to the right of him.

Remember, the object is to get four of the same card in your four-card hand.

So, the dealer draws a card, giving him five, and then slides one over—face down—to the player on his left. The dealer keeps drawing cards one at a time and then sliding one over to the player on his left. He can go as fast or as slow as he wants, thus deciding the tempo of the game.

The player on the dealer's left, who was slid the card the dealer didn't want, takes it into his hand as his fifth card, then slides the one he doesn't want to the player on *his* left. Each player does the same thing, picking up and sliding cards, until the last player, on the right of the dealer, simply makes a new stack of cards next to the deck the dealer is drawing from.

This continues until somebody, through cycling cards in and out, gets four of a kind. The player to get four of the same card first picks up a spoon. When all the others see that someone grabbed a spoon, they make a mad dash to grab the remainders. The player left without a spoon is the loser, and the players who have a spoon but didn't get four of a kind are the semilosers. The semilosers drink half as much as the loser drinks. For instance, if the dealer decided prior to the game that the loser will drink ten drinks, the semilosers all drink five. They are semilosers because, although they got a spoon, they weren't good enough to get four of a kind first. This is to make sure players don't just sit around until they see someone grab a spoon.

There is no reason the dealer can't be the loser or a semiloser. He just has an advantage by seeing the new cards before the others, and cheating whenever possible.

If two people get four of a kind and grab a spoon at the same time, either vote to see who was the fastest, or just say they are both winners or both semilosers.

If you go through the whole deck and nobody has gotten four of a kind yet, start using the deck that the person to the right of the dealer was building. Also, if you make through the entire deck and nobody's gotten four of a kind, try playing Go Fish; it's probably more your caliber.

Alex's Moderately Fun Variations:

- If you get four of a kind first, try to grab a spoon as subtly as possible so no one notices and pretend to keep playing and laugh to yourself as they all try to win even though they're already at least semilosers. That, or grab the spoon and start whacking people with it. I mean, why not?
- If you all think you're all really good (P.S. you aren't), try to play with two less spoons than there are players and have two full losers and fewer semilosers.
- Caution—only for the hard core: One spoon. One winner. Drink up, losers.

Alex's Super-Happy Fun-Time Variation: Change the game's name to Beers and replace the spoons with unopened cans of your favorite booze. The first person to get four of a kind grabs a beer, opens it, and starts chugging. When the others see this, they grab the remaining beers and do the same. This way, if you're a champion chugger, you can still be the winner even if you didn't get four of a kind. The loser who didn't get a beer is in charge of replenishment.

THREE MAN

Booze Slogans!!!

Tequila: Relieving guys the hassle of trying to get a girl's clothes off.

Whiskey: Taking the place of painful memories since 1405.

Drinking Games: Because "eighteen games of Beer Pong" is an excuse for anything.

Alcoholism: The only word that doesn't exist before age twenty-four.

Players: As many as you want. Seriously, the more the better, as long as you don't get easily distracted by all the side chatter and cleavage.

Supplies:

- Two dice
- Something to roll the dice onto

Beer: I'd say just one twenty-four-case, but since the game is called *Three* Man . . .

Objective: There's no objective; you just roll the dice and drink. There's also no winning or losing, unless you consider drinking a lot winning, in which case you'll be the gold medalist of a lifetime. (Note: Gold medals do not prevent whiskey dick.)

Get Your Roll On: Everybody sits around a table and take turns rolling both dice at the same time. If your roll makes someone drink, you keep rolling. To make somebody drink you have to roll, with the two dice combined, five, seven, eleven, or doubles, or have either die be a three.

It's called Three Man because every time somebody rolls the

dice and one or both of them are a three, the Three Man drinks one. You become the Three Man by rolling, with the two dice, a two and a one. If you add those together, it makes three. You are now the Three Man. Congratulations. We'll start pooling bail money in the morning.

There is, of course, a fun and random song you all have to make up before the game starts, and whenever there is a new Three Man, you all must drunkenly belt it out. It should involve a Neanderthal melody and clapping. You can also only use the following words: *da, na,* and *HEY!* for the ending. Good luck with that.

If you roll doubles, you get to hand out the dice to other players to roll. You can give both to the same person or one to each. They then roll these, and drink whatever they roll. *However,* if they roll doubles, you then have to roll both dice again and drink *double* whatever you roll. Unless of course you roll doubles *again,* thus making them roll and drink *triple* whatever they roll. You get the idea.

Your turn keeps going as long as you make somebody drink with each roll. This includes if doubles come back to you. If you get to five rolls in a row (each making somebody drink), you get to make a rule that must be followed for the rest of the game. Like, "You have to grab your crotch whenever you drink or you lose an article of clothing." Or whatever.

This is how the rest of the rolls work:

1 and 1: Doubles

2 and 1: You are the new Three Man. Everybody sings but you. Now drink up, Three Man!

2 and 2: Doubles

3 and 1: The Three Man drinks.

3 and 2: (5 to the right) The person to your right drinks one. The Three Man also drinks.

4 and 1: (5 to the right)

3 and 3: Doubles. Also, Three Man drinks two. It's funny to also give the Three Man the dice to roll because he is the Three Man and is therefore only eligible for certain basic human rights.

4 and 2: Nothing. Pass the die.
5 and 1: Nothing. Pass the die.
6 and 1: (7 to the left) The person to your left drinks one.
5 and 2: (7 to the left)
4 and 3: (7 to the left) Also, the Three Man drinks one.
4 and 4: Doubles
5 and 3: Three Man
6 and 2: Nothing. Pass the die.
5 and 4: Nothing. You suck.
6 and 3: Three Man
5 and 5: Doubles
6 and 4: Nothing. Learn how to roll, douche bag.
5 and 6: Choose someone to drink one.
6 and 6: Do I really need to say what happens here?

Most Likely Dumb Ideas by Alex:

- It's fun if everybody teams up against one person and watches him get faded and pass out and then paint his face like a Ninja Turtle. It's also fun to try to secretly plan things with someone else right under everyone else's nose, like a bank heist or occupation of a third-world country.

- Have a Three Man "hat" with something embarrassing or insulting written on it. All the more reason to not want to be the Three Man. Empty eighteen-packs work well, and can also be lit on fire (by the way).

- If you're daring or nobody's getting drunk fast enough, make a Four Man. Or just double the amount that everyone has to drink. Or inject your veins with rum—but be careful: having a Four Man could be dangerous.

Sing Along! "Da na na dada na na dada na na da na na na da na na—(*CLAP!*)—da na na na dada na na dada na na da na na na da na na na na—*HEY!*"

QUARTERS

Why Not Nickels? Nickels suck. Pennies are cool because they are the absolute smallest American currency and are fun to flick at people. Dimes are just valuable enough to be worth keeping, and quarters are easy to bounce and start the laundry. Nickels are worth too little to carry them around, are unreasonably thick, and ever since 7-Eleven got rid of five-cent candies, they have become completely worthless.

Players: Three or more. Let's not try to get more than ten, though. I mean, come on.

Supplies:

- One quarter
- A cup. The bigger the cup, the greater the challenge (and the bragging rights).
- Tenacity, which Webster helpfully reminds us is, "The quality of being tenacious"

Beer: Just like my old kindergarten teacher used to say, "Drinking is sharing, especially if it gets you laid." Heeding her simple mantra, let's all pitch in some booze and never let our liver get used to any one kind of drink.

Objective: To bounce the quarter into the cup. Nothing funny here.

Starting the Laundry: The only game more simple than Quarters is "1-2-3 Drink," where people take turns saying, "One, two, three, drink," and then drinking a drink on "three." That game, though, is reserved for moments of severe desperation, like when the voices in your head say you need to reach a blood alcohol content of 0.15 percent in sixty seconds or they'll start punching your brain and singing Ted Nugent. But you've all been there; no need to explain that.

Anyway, fill the chosen cup halfway with beer or another alcoholic drink. Sit around a table and take turns trying to bounce the quarter off the table and into the cup (see illustration on page 26 for how to best bounce a quarter). If you make the quarter in, you choose somebody to chug down the cup-o-joy, and then get both the cup and quarter back for another bounce. If you miss the cup, you pass the quarter to the next person for his turn. If you make it in five times in a row, you can make a rule, and should also get a larger cup.

Of course I have other suggestions; I wrote the fucking book . . . Unless you're a goldfish in the body of a human, you will learn how to bounce a quarter fairly well in about three minutes. Therefore, you should either (a) start playing with a dime and graduated cylinder, or (b) try out some of my super-excellent ideas, four of which I slowly typed below:

- Play with a dime and graduated cylinder. Yes, this counts as one of them.
- Bank Shot: This is where the quarter must always be banked off something before landing in the cup. However you make it in, the person you decide to slide the cup to has to make it in the same way. It's like playing H-O-R-S-E but only going to *H.* Popular examples of bank shots include:
    - Off the wall and into the cup
    - Off your well-positioned forehead
    - Off a beer bottle
    - Off the ceiling (yes, it's possible)
- Double Quarters: Players take turns bouncing until they make both of them in. If the quarters are touching each other at the

bottom of the glass, the player gets to hand it to someone to drink. If the quarters are not touching, the player gets to drink it down himself. If the quarters are on top of each other, tackle someone.

- Q-U-A-R-T-E-R-S: Bust out the trick shots and go in an order just as you would while playing the basketball game H-O-R-S-E. Each time you get a letter, you arrange for the glass's interior contents to meet your stomach. My favorite shot? The Double Butt Cheek Squeeze-and-Bounce.

Fine, one more . . .

- Quarter Basketball: Create the outline of a basketball court, using masking tape. Set up two cups on books at either end. Divide into two teams. The teams take turns bouncing the quarter down the court, getting four bounces per turn, trying to get the quarter into the cup, thus scoring two points. Make a three-point line. Reward free throws if the other team commits a (party) foul. For each point scored against you, drink one.

BULL MOOSE

Family History: The little-known cousin of Bull Moose, Bull Cow, is filing charges against her younger cousin for copyright infringement, claiming Bull Moose stole her bouncing quarters into an ice tray idea. Moose says this is bullshit.

Players: Three or more. You can practice on your own, but some call this alcoholism.

Supplies:

- A tall cup or small bucket
- A quarter
- A regular ice tray

Beer: Enough to make you use those moose antlers on your Uncle Herbert's wall for potentially illegal or sexually graphic purposes. And to buy a video camera and stamps to send the footage to Alex Bash.

Moose's Motives: Bounce the quarter into the highest slot possible in the left side of the ice tray, but not into the bucket. Unless you're trying to get "rammed by the bull" (a.k.a. "hammered"—clever, huh?).

Bull's Basics: Set up the ice tray so it's leaning on the bucket just like a ladder leans on a house, or a sloshed incoming freshmen leans on a senior. Each player takes turns trying to bounce the quarter into the ice tray (see illustration on page 26 for how to best bounce a quarter). If you don't get the quarter into one of the slots in the ice tray for whatever reason, you drink three, pass the quarter along, and slide the tray over so it's facing the next player.

If you get it into one of the ice cube slots on the left, you get to hand out that many drinks to whomever you want. The slots are numbered like this: the lowest slot closest to the table is worth one, the next highest is two, then three . . . the highest one is worth seven (usually). You can also split up the drinks between people. For example, if you make it into the sixth-highest slot on the left, you could hand out three drinks to Bob and three to Joe. Or, more realistically, three to Bob's sober self and three to his soon-to-be-drunk-because-he-has-no-tolerance self.

If you make it into a slot on the right, *you* drink the amount it's worth (the drinks are the same as the left side). You only get one bounce per turn unless nobody is paying attention, in which case you should practice your dunking skills.

If you make it into the highest slot on either side, not only do you get to either hand out or drink seven, you also make a rule that everybody must follow for the rest of the game. If you are trying for the highest slot to make a rule and overbounce the quarter into the bucket, you must finish your whole drink, you egotistical jerk.

The whole reason the game is called Bull Moose is because when the quarter goes into either of the top two ice cube slots, everybody has to put both their hands on their head imitating a moose's antlers and yell, "Bull moose!" Don't ask why. Just accept it. The last one to do so drinks five big ones.

Rules in this game are hilarious because everybody is always so focused on the ice cube tray that no one follows them. Call them out on them as often as possible. Even you, Bull Cow—I don't care what your lawyers say.

CARD GAMES!!!

31

31's Medical Report: "Thirty-one has developed severe multiple-personality . . . ness," said Alex Bash, MD, speaking from his fraternity, Pi Kappa Alpha. "Sometimes he is his regular '31'self, but every now and then he'll slip into his personality of Thirty-One where he completely disregards the number pad on his keyboard. On Mondays, he thinks he's a Roman warrior and calls himself XXXI, which is somewhat hard to understand, seeing as how he doesn't even *speak* Roman. Lastly, on weekends he becomes Spanish and claims to be Spain and Mexico's illegitimate child, Spexico. Apparently, this makes sense while drunk; I'll research later tonight."

Players: Between two and six works well; also, between six and two.

Supplies: A deck of cards. You could use a trick deck, but the game might not work that well.

Wine: Ha! Just kidding. A twelve-pack should do. Something heavy.

Objective: To make your hand add up to as close to thirty-one as possible

Basics: Everyone starts with three cards in his hand. Player One (the person with the largest nostrils) draws a card from the deck and then discards one face up into the discard pile next to the deck. Player Two can either draw from the deck or pick up the top card on the discard pile.

Important: You can only ever pick up the very top card on the discard pile. If the card you want is buried, too bad. It's gone.

You can only ever have three cards in your hand at the end of your turn (start with three, draw one, and then discard one; it's like math, or something).

Scoring your hand: All numbered cards are worth their face value (a five=5 points, a nine=9 points); jacks, queens, and kings are each worth ten; and aces are worth eleven. *But,* cards in your hand only add up together in points if they are the same suit. For example, if your hand consists of the jack of clubs, the five of clubs, and the ace of diamonds, your hand is worth fifteen points (jack=10, five=5). The ace is not counted because it is not a club. It's also only worth eleven, which is less than your clubs. You always make your best hand possible, unless you choose to waive your three kings and pass out under the table.

In the case that someone does pass out under the table, that person's beer is officially considered "social" and can be drunk by anyone. My roommate just thought of that; blame him.

When you think you have a better hand than anyone else, you knock on the table. If the table opens, then someone put LSD in your beer. On the turn in which you knock, you cannot draw a card. Everyone else gets one more turn before all the players show what they have. Assuming you win, each player with a lower hand drinks one drink for every point he has less than you. So, if you knocked with twenty-eight points, Bob had twenty-five, and Joe had twenty-three, Bob would drink three and Joe would drink five. If at any point in the game you get thirty-one in your hand (an ace and two ten-pointers of the same suit), you lay it down and the game is over. You win. Now go hook up.

The game keeps going around until someone knocks or gets thirty-one. If you go through the entire deck and nobody has knocked or got thirty-one, then (a) you all suck, and (b) the game is over. Show your cards and finish all your beer. Morons.

If the player who knocked does not have the highest hand, he drinks double how many points he is behind the leader, because he's like that guy who always thinks he's the best at something until he shoots the football through the hoop and pees himself before passing out in Tri Delt's side yard.

If you knock, and in the last turn one of the other players gets thirty-one, you still drink double however many behind you are from thirty-one. Should have heard that one knocking, genius.

If you manage to get three of a kind, your hand is worth thirty. Feel free to knock. Trying to get three of a kind can be very risky though because if you only get two of the three needed, your hand will most likely be quite low. This strategy works best with cards like twos and threes, because everyone always discards them.

Try this game playing to forty-one, and have four cards in your hand at all times. Now, four of a kind is worth forty but is *very* hard to get. Playing to fifty-one and sixty-one work but, let me tell you—going for six of a kind is really fucking hard.

One Last Textually Confusing Thought . . . : Turkey produces more grapes than Chile. Think about it.

ACROSS THE BRIDGE

Signs You May Have Imbibed too Much:

- You have an argument with the lamp. And lose.
- You yell at the doctors pumping your stomach, "Hey, that was Grey Goose!"
- The whole bar says, "Hi, Jim!" when you walk in—your name is George.
- You play every game in Alex Bash's *Imbible* in one night . . . twice.

A Player: Is usually someone with multiple girlfriends. You'll need two to play.

Supplies: A deck of cards, maybe two

Beer: Try drinking your beer out of an odd object, like a vase or puncture wound.

Objective: To make your way across the bridge, getting as few face cards as possible

Getting Across: Each person lays the top ten cards from the deck face down, going from you to the person sitting across from you. Keep the remaining deck close by. Take turns turning over one card at a time until someone reaches the end of the line he laid out. When either person reaches the end, you each count your face cards and whoever has the least wins. The loser drinks double the amount of face cards the winner has, so if Bob had seven face cards and Jack had five, Bob would drink ten. Sorry, Bob.

So, each turn you flip over the first card in front of you; if it's a two through a ten, your turn is over. If the card is a jack, queen, king, or ace, you have to do the following: lick your shoe.

Just kidding.

If the card is a . . .

Jack: You drink one, and lay down one more card from the deck at the end of your line.

Queen: You drink two, and lay down two more cards from the deck at the end of your line.

King: You drink three, and lay down three more cards from the deck at the end of your line.

Ace: You drink four, and lay down four more cards from the deck at the end of your line.

Joker: You drink ten and kick yourself in the face, Batman.

You *keep* the face card that you turn over for the end of game tally. When you draw a face card (bad luck), you have two options. The first, and most common, is to drink the designated number of drinks and lay down that number of cards. You then must make it through the next one through four cards *without* getting another face card, or else you drink *double* what it was originally worth, keep the face card, and your turn is over.

Option two is for the larger-testicled man . . . or woman: you can go double-or-nothing on both the drinks and the face cards. This means that if you draw a face card, you can choose to turn over the next one through four cards (depending on the face card's value) and, if none of them are face cards, you are acquitted of all drinks *as well as* get to discard the original face card you drew. However, if any one of them is a face card, you owe double the number of drinks originally owed, and you must go through the deck and find a second face card to give yourself. Nice one, Mr. Brave Man.

You may also do a "triple-or-nothing," whereby everything is the same except the number of cards is tripled, the drinks are tripled, and the extra face cards given are tripled. This is both mathematically stupid as well as generally stupid; in other words, it's perfect for drinking games. You may also, as a group, decide whether you have this option, because it can kind of get out of control if someone keeps pulling kings and aces. And by out of control, I of course mean extremely-fucking-awesome.

If you get to the end of the bridge during a double-or-nothing challenge, you must shuffle the previously used cards and continue to lay more down. Nice try, cheapo.

If it's summer, try playing on an actual bridge, and have the allotted drinks equal the number of seconds the player needs to pee on a boat passing beneath. Sorry, Mr. Allen, I lost a triple-down.

Again.

ASSHOLE

Tips for the Drunken Asshole: You are *not* a badass. No, you cannot jump those stairs on your bike. You don't even own a bike. That's the neighbor's dog. And you're peeing on it. And no, the grass was not yelling at you and you don't need to elbow-drop it from the third-story balcony. The second story will be plenty high enough. Yes, from atop the railing. Cameras ready!

Players: As many as you like

Supplies:

- A deck of cards and an empty stomach . . . and liver
- A fully functioning navy. This could get intense.

Beer: Whatever the Beer Bitch brings you (this will make sense later)

Objective: Get rid of your cards first, bang the secretary, and liberate a third-world country from oppression before lunch. Sometimes pass laws. And we can't forget Conspiracy Fridays!

Presidential Decrees: Read them now, so I can use the terms while explaining and justify typing *asshole* as often as possible.

President: The President can make anybody drink whenever he wants. Don't abuse it *too much* or, next round, you'll get what's coming to you (low memoir sales).

Vice President: Must ask, after everything the President says, "But, sir, is that rational!?" and sound overly alarmed. If he fails, he drinks one. He can make anybody except the President drink whenever he wants. He also doesn't really have to follow that first rule, or you'd all suffer annoyance-induced aneurysms.

Secretary: Must repeat the last word in each sentence the President says, as if writing it down. He *does* have to follow this rule. If possible, make a motion as if typing. If he fails, he drinks one. This position can make anybody below him drink whenever he wants.

Asshole: The Asshole must deal and clear the cards each round and drink whenever anybody says he must; however, he can make anybody drink as much as he likes as he is shuffling and dealing. This is the only chance you get, Asshole, so use it wisely.

Beer Bitch: The second-to-lowest rank is the Beer Bitch. In this case, it would be the Secretary, but would change if more players joined. The Beer Bitch is responsible for getting every player new beers, and refilling drinks upon request.

Tickling the Butt: Deal all the cards out evenly. Whoever has the three of clubs plays first by laying it down face up on the table. The next person must then lay down a card equal to or higher than the three. Suit doesn't matter. Turns keep going around the table with players taking turns rapidly firing away into the ever-growing pile of what are most likely wrinkled '80s Playboy cards or cheap promotional cards for the latest *Pirates* movie. Spilled beer can join, too.

The card you play must always be higher than the one before

yours. If someone doesn't have a single card higher than the person before, he may play a pair of cards. The next person must then lay down a higher pair of cards. If he cannot play, he is skipped. He does not have to pick up the stack of cards or anything like that; he just misses out on laying down some cards from his hand, the point, of course, being to lay them all down first.

You can*not* lay down other hands from poker like flushes, straights, or full houses; stick to pairs, three of a kind, and four of a kind. If you ever get five of a kind, you fucked up.

At anytime, a two of any suit clears the pile (on your turn, of course). These are good to save until the end or for when you're stuck. Therefore, threes are the lowest possible cards, twos the best, and aces are second best. If the turn goes around the whole table and no one can play because Mr. Tough Guy laid down three kings, the pile is cleared as if a two was played and Mr. Tough Guy goes again.

Real quick: If you lay down the same card as the person before you, the next player's turn is skipped. If the next person then lays down the same card *again,* the next *two* people's turns are skipped.

Summary: the game goes around the table, each person laying down between one and four cards at a time from his hand, always equal to or higher than the player before him. If no one can match or beat FagMo's played cards, FagMo gets to clear them and play again.

Now that you know what cards are good and bad, here's this: Before the game begins, the President gives the Asshole his two worst cards (a three and a four, for example, because two threes would be a pair), and the Asshole gives the President his two best cards (either twos or a high pair). If it turns out he is lying, he's automatically the Asshole again next game; you'll notice halfway through the game if he's lying when he lays down three aces.

Important: If at any point in the game you can make all four of a certain card stacked on top of the pile, you can lay them down, clear it, and go again. Let me explain: If you're not next in line to lay down cards, but the person across from you laid down two jacks, and you have the other two jacks in your hand, before the next person plays, you can slap down those two jacks and steal the turn! You can also do this by laying three-of-a-kind on one or one on three-of-a-kind. If one of the deck's four cards has been played in a previous round and only three are left, you can't do this (obviously). This strategy keeps people focused and as quick minded as they can be after a pint of Bacardi Gold.

Senator Douche: If more than five people want to play, you have to give them government names like Secretary of Defense or Chief Staffing Officer or House Representative or whatever. Also, give them tasks to do, like the Vice and Secretary. Advice: Any position-related task involving drinking heavily, saying stupid shit, or carrying out embarrassing dances is always fun.

Tip from the Oval Office: Make sure to keep track of the duties of each position and to always let the Asshole know just how much of an Asshole he is. We're all about self-esteem around here.

The Fifth Term: In the real world, presidents get forced out of office too early to make any lasting impact because the next Yale-educated white Christian male just repeals whatever he set in place. In Asshole, once you get to your fifth term, you get to make a rule that will never be repealed—ever. My favorite is: Hippies always triple the amount they have to drink, in hopes of killing themselves off early. But you can choose your own, too.

BEERQUAKE 10.5

News Reporter: *"We have a major emergency on our hands here, Tom! It's a BeerQuake 10.5 on the Richter scale, which may be slightly skewed because Richter just played nineteen games of Speed Quarters but still, scary stuff! There's lukewarm beer everywhere! Unrefrigerated Busch Light spewing from the walls, shooting up from the ground! It's only a matter of time before we're boning fat chicks and singing along to 'American Pie'!"*

Players: However many survivors you can garner up

Supplies:

- Cards, and, if you're lacking what some call "normal brain activity," a calculator may help
- BeerQuake Band-Aids (Gatorade)

Beer: 10.5 beers should do.

Objective: Get closer to 10.5 than the dealer without going over. Look out for beer magma (warm beer; horrific).

Avoiding the Quake: This game is basically a screwed-up version of blackjack. To start 10.5, remove all the eights, nines, and red tens from the deck; leave the black tens. Whoever has the longest hair starts as dealer; just accept it, you girly man. The dealer deals one card face down to each person including himself. Everybody looks at his respective card without showing anybody else, except for the dealer, who keeps his card face up. Don't even try to hide it behind your hair.

Each player plays independently with the dealer, just as in blackjack. Yes, you are playing at the same table and against the dealer and may cheer for one another, but what Bob gets compared to Joe doesn't affect each other's hand. The turns go clockwise, starting with the person to the left of the dealer.

Before Player One's turn, he bets a number of drinks. If in the end he beats the dealer, the dealer drinks that many; but if Player One loses, he drinks his own bet. So Player One looks at his card and chooses whether he wants another card (a "hit") or if he is satisfied with what he has (to "stay"). He never shows anybody else any of his cards until everybody, including the dealer, has had a turn. Player One's goal, as stated earlier, is to get his hand as close to equaling 10.5 as possible *without* going over. If your hand becomes worth more than 10.5 (called "busting"), you must declare this fact and drink your drinks. Go play slots.

This is what cards are worth:

10: Wild. Say it's your first card, make it worth 10.5, and "stay" because you're probably gonna win. If you hit twice and your three-card hand equals 7, and *then* you get a 10, make it worth 3.5. Obviously the best card in the deck.

Face Card: Jack, queen, and king are each worth 0.75 points.

Ace: An ace is worth 1.25 points.

2–7: Any card between two and seven is worth its face value. A seven can make or break your hard.

So, Player One has his turn, and hits, stays, or busts. When he is satisfied or busted, it's Player Two's turn. Same thing continues around the table to the dealer. The dealer is just like a regular player except that whatever he gets determines what everybody else does, unless of course they've already busted. The dealer must turn over his cards face up as he hits or stays, to make it more intense. Everybody else has already gone, so it doesn't matter if his hand is seen.

Keep in mind: The dealer has no idea what the unbusted players have and therefore doesn't know when to stop hitting. It's up to him to decide when he thinks he probably has the majority of the other players beaten. For example, say he thinks 9.25 is a solid hand and declares that he's "staying" and then the unbusted players all turn over 9.5s and 10s; he has to drink the combined bets of everybody who beat him. If the dealer ever busts, he must drink all the unbusted players' drinks. So, unlike in blackjack, the dealer can stop hitting whenever he wants to.

A Little More Ish:

- Take turns being the dealer. It just goes around the table clockwise. If you want to be a bitch, you could do it to where, unless the dealer beats a majority of the other players, he is still the dealer.
- The reason all the cards are worth odd numbers like .75 is to mess with you, especially as you get drunk. I remember (was reminded about) playing poker once with some buddies and doing well until my friend brought me a fifth of Fireball whiskey and a large glass of ice. I ended up pushing all my chips in on an inside-straight draw. I lost.
- If you feel the numbers are too confusing, feel free to change the values. Also, feel free to retake fourth grade.

Remember . . . The greater the balls, the greater the glory, the greater the story to tell your parents why you fed the dog Fritos.

BEER 99

This game stemmed from the infamous drinking song "Ninety-nine Bottles of Beer on the Wall." The song was a simple, fun way to get slammed until that little shit Mickey took seat #1 and passed oral herpes and mono to 75 percent of Europe. Some call it the Black Plague; I call it "The Biggest Party Foul *Ever.*"

Players: Four or more. Maybe 4½ if you're crazy. Chainsaw crazy.

Supplies:
- A deck of cards
- The ability to lie to your friends, the way Mickey did when he discovered the sores in his mouth and traded seats with a poor little rat and blamed it on him. Rats have been seen as dirty ever since. So sad, so sad.

Beer: Enough to sooth your soon-to-be-aching head

Objective: To play the card that brings the pile's total to exactly ninety-nine

Basics: Deal four cards to everybody. No one is the dealer and no one has an advantage over anybody. You go around the circle, playing one card face up in a pile in the middle and drawing one every time you play one, so you always have four cards in your hand at once.

Throughout the game, keep track in your head what the pile is worth; the total value, if you will. This will determine whether you win or lose. Here's the value of the cards:

2–9: Face value
10: Positive 10 or negative 10. You must declare aloud which one you choose when you lay it down. If the pile is at 90 or higher, it is always worth negative 10.
Jack: 11
Queen: 12
King: 13
Ace: 1 or 14. Again, you've got to say it aloud which one you choose.

The goal is to be the person who lays down the card to make the pile worth ninety-nine, so you need to keep track of what it's at and pace yourself and make sure others can't get there after your turn.

Important: If a player makes the pile worth more than ninety-nine, he drinks three and the pile's value returns to eighty. This can be a strategy for either winning or getting the player who goes after you drunk. If you land on ninety-nine, congratulations! You can hand out fifteen drinks to whomever you want.

As you play, there are a few special numbers and events to take note of:

Anything ending in 9: Whenever the pile equals a number ending in 9, everybody drinks two.

If it lands on 69 or 71: You all drink three. Don't ask, just drink.

If a card is laid on top of the same card: that second card is doubled. A third same card adds triple its usual amount, and a fourth duplicate adds a quadrupled amount to the pile. So, if the pile is worth 10, and you lay down a five, it's now worth 15, like normal. But if another five is laid down on top of the first one, it's now worth 25, get it? The second five is worth 10?

Also important: When laying down a card, you must completely cover up the previous one so only the very top card (your card) is showing at any given time. This makes it more difficult to keep track of the pile's total. When the pile lands on ninety-nine, the winner hands out his drinks and you start again at zero.

Note: Ninety-nine 1-ounce swigs is only 8.25 Beers.

Strategies:

- You can try, if daring, to bluff your drunken friends. Say you know the pile equals ninety-four but you don't have a five, you have a four. You can lay the four down and declare ninety-nine. If the others are too scared to contradict you, you win! If you get caught, whatever, you'll probably be too drunk to remember it.

- People always think there's going to be some dispute as to whether the pile is actually worth ninety-nine or whatever. This rarely happens, as usually at least two or three people are smart enough and know what it's at. If not, you can always go back through and count aloud together the cards laid down in succession. Note: This is also how you catch someone bluffing.
- If everyone goes through his entire hand and no one makes the pile equal 99, then just remember the pile's total, shuffle it up, and deal it back out evenly.
- To encourage bluffing/lying: if someone lays down a card and says, "Ha! Ninety-nine, bitches!" and another player doesn't believe him, it's on the doubter to prove him wrong. If the doubter is correct in his doubting ways, the bluffer drinks fifteen. If the doubter is wrong, he drinks twenty and you get to clown on him for having deep-seated trust issues.
- If you think this sounds too confusing for a drinking game, just think back to that eighth-grade geometry test you took after playing Pass-the-Half-G in the locker room after PE! Am I right?! No? Just me? Really? Damn . . . the counselors were right . . .

BEERAMID

A conspiracy tracing back millennia. The pyramids of Giza. King Tut's demise. The eye in the temple on the dollar bill. Secret caverns under the Library of Congress. JFK. The Pentagon Papers. The fake moon landing.

Jay Leno's chin.

Minds will be blown when it all comes together as you turn over the last two rows of cards in Beeramid, and drink double the usual amount. Now wake up—you passed out under the couch again watching *The Da Vinci Code.*

Players: A few*

Supplies:

- A deck of playing cards
- Basic geometric abilities

Alcohol:

- Franzia
- Hangover medicine

Note: Beeramid got its name not from being shaped like a pyramid, but because it was invented by Giorgio Beer de Amid. Go figure.

Objective: To lie to your trusted friends and get them drunk. This game is also used as a training course for corporate America's up-coming executives. Ooooo—burn!

Climbing the Beeramid: Lay fifteen cards face down in the shape of a pyramid (5-4-3-2-1) and deal five cards face down to each player. Or, to mess with someone, "accidentally" flip one over as you pass it to him. Sucker. Everybody looks at his respective cards.

Then somebody, doesn't matter who, turns over the bottom left card of the pyramid. If you have a card of the same value in your hand, you announce it and get to hand out three drinks. You do *not* show anyone your card. Other players can call you out if they don't think you have it. They may have a hunch, or

* Few = three to six people

they might have the other three cards in their own hand. Good one.

If you get your bluff correctly called, you (the bluffer) drink double what that card was worth (six). If someone incorrectly calls out your bluff, he (the doubter) drinks triple (nine). This is to encourage bluffing (a.k.a. "lying with a smile").

If you have two of the overturned cards in your hand, declare it aloud and hand out double the drinks (six). If you have three of the overturned card, call it and hand out three times the drinks. If you get called out on multiple cards, the drink total is still doubled (six becomes twelve). So if someone turns over a king, you say, "I got two kings; drink six, fucker." But if Joe, who *actually* has two kings in his hand and therefore knows you are lying says, "Bullshit, mofo, I'm callin' you out," you'd have to drink twelve. Joe should also drink twelve for saying "mofo."

After each card is turned over, it gets turned back down again and you continue on up the pyramid to the top. This is in hopes of players' forgetting what has already been turned over. By now you should have, if you've been keeping track, a pretty good idea of what is in each person's hand. It's like that card game memory, the memory of which you are slowly drinking away, making more free space in your brain for movie quotes.

One last thing: In the top two rows (two cards and one), all drinks are doubled. So if you have the turned-over card in your hand, you hand out six; if you get called out for bluffing, you drink twelve; and incorrectly calling someone out earns you eighteen big ones, mofo.

Slight Variations:

- If you get too good, try playing with two decks so there's eight of each card floating around.
- To get drunker, make cards in the first row worth three drinks; the next row, six; the next row, nine; then twelve; and then

fifteen for the Beeramid's spire. *Then* play with two decks. Have your camera phones ready.

You'd be surprised how much you can get for blackmail photos these days.

BLOW JOB!

Now that I have your attention, I can address an important issue. Over the years, many awkward times have come between men when they "cheers" their beers. This is because no one knows whether to tilt it back and cheers the bottom of the bottle or tilt it forward and cheers the top. From now on, always cheers the bottom because (a) if your beer is full, tilting it forward will spill precious beer onto your friend—not cool; (b) the part of the bottle that has touched both your lips will touch, which is entirely too gay; and (c) if you tilt it back, you're already halfway to pouring it into your mouth.

Now, how about that fellatio.

Players: Hell, you could play this by yourself, if you want.

Supplies:

- A tall glass filled with beer, with an opening smaller than a deck of cards
- A deck of cards
- No teeth

Beer: Enough to fill the glass and have enough left over to accidentally spill on Melissa's tank top

Blow Job: (*noun, slang; vulgar*) An act or instance of fellatio

Objective: To blow one card off the top of the deck at a time

Unzipping the Pants: Before you start the game, everybody pick a suit. I'll explain later.

Set the entire deck of cards on top of the beer-filled glass. Set the glass in the middle of whatever table you're playing on, so everyone is the same distance away. Take turns trying to blow one and only one card off the top of the deck. If you succeed in blowing only one card off the top, you get to hand out two drinks to whomever you want. If you blow off more than one, you drink two.

After one card or more falls off, it's the next person's turn. Leave the cards where they fall, face up or face down. When the game is over, everybody (yes, even the winner) has to drink one for every blown-off card that's facing up of the suit each player chose before the game. Just one more way to wrap that beer blanket tighter around you.

Whoever blows off the remaining card gets to drink the glass the cards were sitting on. Yes, even if there's only one card left. Obviously, your friends are good at blowing (cards). Drink up.

If you like, you can play to where no one can lean forward and blow (unlike blowing other things . . . like wet paint). Now, everyone must just sit upright in his chair and blow from several feet away. *Way* harder, and also makes the game go quicker so you can move onto other acts that involve blowing, like blowing out those long, hard, throbbing candles before they burn the house down.

BULLIES

The World Is a Beer Aisle: At the bottom, you have the cases: twenty-four cheap beers fresh out of the brewery (college) and willing to be put to less important tasks (Beer Pong vs. elite company function). All companies (people) get them, some get fired (spilled, left over), and all are dispensable but necessary. Then there's the bullies. The "nice six-packs." The CEOs of Beer World—they cost more, but do less. They sit atop the cases and eighteeners smiling deviously behind their $12.99 price tags (salary), only willing to go down to $11.99 with a Safeway Club Card Discount (tax write-offs, backdated stock options). Cheap beer's only hope is if the all-powerful politicians (kegs) carry them in greater quantities to the most important functions of all (frat parties) and let their voice be heard (keg stands)!

Players: Two could work, but three or more is best.

Supplies: Cards, saliva

Beer: Get a case of college graduates and mix them in a box with CEOs and middle management. We're all about equality, in *The Imbible.*

Objective: To try to get people with high cards to fold by bullying them and then have a higher card than anybody left, all before your card falls off your forehead

Basics: Everybody is dealt a card that he *cannot look at.*

Important: Do not look at your card.

Also important: Read the above statement again.

After not looking at your card like a good Imbiber, lick the back of it and stick it to your forehead. If at any time your card falls off your head, you lose and have to drink three. You may not touch your card after you have stuck it to your forehead, but may lean your head back all you want to try to keep it from falling off, although you may look retarded.

Once you all stick your card to your head *without looking at it* (don't cheat, fucker), you try to get other people to back out of the round by persuading them that your card is higher than theirs. The highest card is an ace, the lowest is a two; if two people have the same highest card, they both win. You only have a limited amount of time to convince people to fold before your card falls off. If you fold your card, you do not have to drink anything; you are just a pussy.

Once you've all decided who is staying in the hand, you bring your cards down and reveal the winner. The player with the highest card hands out ten drinks to whomever he wants (including those who folded), and everybody who stayed in the hand and lost drinks three on top of whatever the winner gives him.

Bullying Techniques:

- After a quick glance around at one another's cards, a few of you may want to try to work together to get out the guy who has the ace, but if he realizes that everybody is bullying him he'll know he has a high card. You could also throw some reverse psychology at the guy with a high card, so he thinks his card sucks and folds his would-be winning card.

- If you are indeed dudes, I know it's easy to be all badass and stay in every single round regardless of what's happening and be like, "Dude, I don't even care; I'm crazy; I wanna drink." Yes, we all know you are tough but, just like sneaking a peak at your own card, it makes the game less fun. And your panties are showing.

- If you get bored, try to convince the drunkest guy that using superglue is a great idea because his card will *never* fall off! Plastic surgery doesn't cost *that* much, right?

BULLSHIT

Caution: This game contains explicit material; I don't mean to type it, my fingers have a mind of their own, and I am truly, deeply sorry, especially if you have a deep-seated traumatic experience involving a bull shitting on you.

Where Does "Bull Shit" Come From? From a bull's ass, moron. Kidding, but not really. From what I read in obscure Google articles, the term *bullshit* originated from a deceitful Irish lawyer named Obadiah Bull. It was first introduced into a dictionary in 1915. And who said a book designed to make you get drunk and start a ketchup fight couldn't be educational?

Players: Three or more. At least one should be a cow, or this could get ugly.

Supplies:
- Hay to eat (munchies)
- A deck of cards
- A barn to sleep in (seriously; no metaphor here)

Beer: A brewski or two could definitely aid in the progression of enjoyable activities

Side Note: Cows are much harder to tip than you think; the average full-grown cow weighs in at 1,400 pounds. You'll need at least four to five strong guys and a girl named Kristina to take the picture. Watch out for poo.

Objective: To get rid of all your cards first

Basics: Deal out the entire deck evenly to all players. Make sure nobody sees anybody else's cards. The person to the left of the dealer starts, play goes clockwise, and you take turns being the dealer. Player One must lay a two face down in the middle of the table. Player Two must then lay down a three, Player Three must then lay down a four, and so on up to jack, queen, king, ace, and then back to two, three, four, and so on. However, the cards are face down and nobody knows if you're really playing the card you say.

Obviously, you will not always have the card you need. If the person before you laid down a nine, and you have no tens, you have to lay a random card face down and say "one ten." This is why it's called Bullshit. A lot (if not most) of the time, people are lying about the cards they lay down. If you think they're lying, or know they are because you have all four of the cards they claim to lay down, you can call, "Bullshit." They then have to turn over the card(s) they just laid down and prove you wrong or right.

If they were indeed bullshitting, they have to pick up the entire pile of cards, which sucks because the point is to get rid of your cards. If they were telling the truth, the doubter has to pick up the pile. This is a game of bluffing and reading people, and is especially difficult to play with strangers because you don't know how to read them.

Drinking! Each time someone gets called out for bluffing, he has to drink two for each card he picks up. If someone incorrectly calls someone out, *he* has to drink two for each card he picks up.

You can also lay down a few cards at a time and say "two fours" or "three tens" or "four kings," and so on. Each time you lay down more than two of any particular card and no one calls you out, you get to hand out five drinks. Let me tell you, though: it's extremely hard to get away with laying down five of anything.

On Being a Little Bitch:

- Don't be afraid to call bullshit on someone; if no one calls it because everybody is scared, then the game will be too easy. You're all bound to get called out at least once, anyway.

- Don't be too disheartened if you have to pick up a pile consisting of half the deck. When you have all the cards, you can always tell if someone's bullshitting and call everyone out until you get back to a reasonable-size hand.

Morality: If someone doesn't feel comfortable saying the word *shit,* it is totally fine. Just make sure to call him "Fuck Face" for the rest of his life.

CARD TOSS

Currency: Everybody flipped out when the European Union's currency surpassed the U.S. dollar in value. Why didn't we care this much when they passed us in cussing? If you go to Europe and start a verbal argument, you'll be blown away. They can insult you so well, you'll forget what you're being insulted for and just feel, well, insulted. Let's change this, America! No more "Screw you" or "You're a dick" or "Fuck you." Let's get creative. Start reading the thesaurus. Try out potential insults on strangers. We'll be on our way to spontaneously glorious cussing in no time, you churlish smudge of unwashed whale semen!

Players: As many rank gobs of petrified penile warts as you can find

Supplies:
- A few decks of cards
- One of those stereotypical magician's hats. (Or just a big mixing bowl or something; a one-foot opening will do.)

Beer: A lot for the game, and a lot for ridiculing the vats of brain dead aardvark discharge (other players)

Official Fruit of Card Toss: The mango. I dunno.

Objective: To toss a card into the hat or bowl. Yup, no metaphor in this title.

Basics: Everybody sits an equal distance from the top hat or mixing bowl. Your distance from the bowl depends on how good you are. The closer you are, the easier it is, but try to sit far enough away so it's pretty hard to get a card in (you should make about one in seven).

It's best to each have your own deck of cards to toss from but, if not, just divide the deck evenly. Players take turns trying to toss the top card of their deck into the hat. You have to take turns to avoid confusion as to whose card made it in, especially when you're drunk.

Important: Everyone chooses a position in the army (corporal, general, soldier, etc.) and then adds his last name. This serves as your name for the rest of this game.

Taking turns, players draw the top card of their deck and call out if it is red or black, and if it's worth ten drinks or five. Cards between two and nine are worth five drinks, and cards ten or above (ten, jack, queen, king, or ace) are worth ten drinks.

My turn would sound like this, "General Bash firing a red-tenner!" I'd then toss my card the best I could into the hat. If I make it, I hand out ten drinks to whomever I please. Turns move on whether you make it or not. It's generally a fast-moving game. Eventually people aren't waiting for their turn and cards just start flying everywhere and players pound beers without even noticing if they have to or not.

"General Bash—permission to get shit-faced, Sir?" "Permission granted, soldier!"

CHUMBAWUMBA

Most people know the word *chumbawumba* from that annoying song about how people fall down but get up again, and whom we apparently will never keep down. But it's more than that: it's the alcoholic's anthem, urging us to keep "working late." To keep "having bad balance." To keep "waking up far from home with no shoes." To keep "regaining consciousness during a liver surgery in a dark alley." If you get knocked down, get back up again! We can do it!

Players: Between 2 and 621. Any more is simply too many.

Supplies:

- Cards. Pretty surprising, seeing as though we're in the "card game" section.
- Beer

Beer: More beer

Official Chumbawumba Anagram: A MAW CHUM BUM

Object: To get rid of all your cards

Basics: Deal out all the cards evenly. Nobody looks at his cards; just hold them all face down in a stack. Takes turns laying down the top card of your stack face up in the middle of the table.

Important: Sounds odd, but you *must* turn the card over from the front (away from you) so that everybody has the same chance to see it first. You can't turn it up toward you so that you see it as you're laying it down; you'll see why.

If a card laid down matches the one right before it (an ace on an ace, a nine on a nine, etc.), everybody must yell, "Chumbawumba!"

The last person to do so picks up the pile of cards and has to drink the following amounts: if the card was a . . .

2–5: Three drinks
6–9: Four drinks
10–Queen: Five drinks
King: Six drinks
Ace: Eight drinks (yes, I skipped seven)

The card must be turned over away from you so you don't have the advantage of seeing it first. When you lay down your last card, you are the winner and the others keep playing for second place, third place, and so on down to 621st place. The game is simple, but so is being punched in the jaw, so be careful.

Potential Chumbawumba Anagrammed Names for Players:

- CUB WUMBA HAM
- MUBBA MAW CHU
- CAB MAW BUM UM
- BA-WUM BA-CHUM
- MACHUM BA WUB
- HA MAW BUB CUM

You're welcome.

CIRCLE OF WONDERFULNESS

The Alcohol Life Cycle—Part 1 of 3: Alcohol, contrary to popular belief, is not asexual. A strong, heavy beer, with at least 7 percent alcohol content, has to win over the heart of a nice, slender Mike's Hard Lemonade or quaint mixed drink and fill it full of metaphorical beer semen. The alcohol egg is then fermented by barley and hops DNA, with the occasional recessive distillation gene. These processes take place up until alcohol's thirteenth birthday, when "beer pressure" begins.

Players: The more players, the less hammered you'll get. Yup, that means playing alone.

Supplies:

- A deck of cards
- At least a C in geometry

Beer: Any amount that could be deemed "in excess of wonderfulness"

Why Aliens Will Never Invade Us: *The Fast and the Furious* is one of the most rented videos of all time. We are obviously an uncivilized race.

Objective: To get around the circle without dying

Basics: Place as many cards face down in a circle as you want. I'd suggest about four or five cards for each player. Take turns guessing if the card you pick up out of the circle will be red or black. If you're correct, you get to hand out the following amount of drinks to whomever you want:

2–10:	Face value
Jack:	Four or eleven
Queen:	Three or twelve
King:	Two or thirteen
Ace:	One or fourteen

If you guess incorrectly, you have to drink however many the card is worth. However, the higher cards are worth minimal drinks to you but much more to others. For example, if you guess the wrong color and draw an ace, you only have to drink one, but if you guess the correct colored ace, you get to hand out fourteen. If you incorrectly guess the color of a jack, you only drink four and not eleven. This is why drawing high cards is good for you and bad for the others. When you draw cards, it does not need to be in any order.

Now, just because your turn is over doesn't mean you're off the hook. You always keep the card you drew on your previous turn. This card is "pending" while Player Two guesses and draws. Regardless of whether Player Two guesses right or wrong, if his card is the same suit as yours, you both have to drink three in addition to whatever drinks Player Two may hand out or have to drink. If this happens, both of your cards are still "pending" until Player Three goes. If *his* card is also the same suit, you all drink six. If Player Four's card is the same suit, you all drink nine. This keeps going around, adding on three drinks each time until the chain of same-suit cards is broken. I've never seen it get to more than twenty-one, and I think people were cheating. Keep in mind that these drinks are all in addition to the ones you already have to drink from your correct or incorrect guess.

If Player Two's card is the same *value* as yours, meaning you drew a nine on your turn and Player Two also drew a nine, you both have to drink ten. This is of course very unlikely. *If* you happen to get a third same card draw in a row, drink twenty. Each. You have the worst luck *ever*. If you are playing with two or more decks (you'll need to with ten or more players) and the *exact* same card (suit *and* value) is drawn in succession, both players involved finish their entire drinks. The game ends when, as a group, you make it around the circle.

Higher Education: For more on *The Imbible*'s original series, "The Alcohol Life Cycle," please turn to Circle of Betterness on the next page. Be prepared to take notes.

CIRCLE OF BETTERNESS

The Alcohol Life Cycle—Part 2 of 3: Beer pressure has different effects on different alcohols. Some alcohols give in and live the beer's miscreant lifestyle of getting bonged, shotgunned, and stuffed into a keg. Other alcohol is strong willed enough to think for itself and become its own beverage, like a fine wine or delicate vodka. But sometimes the beer pressure forces the poor alcohol into hiding, makes it too scared to fully blossom; and it ends up living life as a "bitch beer," guzzled by sorority freshmen and ending up on your floor the next morning.

Players: The more players, the less hammered you'll all get. Yup, that means zero. Figure it out.

Supplies:
- A deck or two of cards
- A working liver
- A one-size-fits-all coffin

Beer: Gonna have to be at least high school grads for this one. The beer, that is.

Objective: To make it around both circles. I'd make a joke about "not dying," but that may actually be possible, so it loses its humor.

Basics: Lay the whole deck of cards face down in a big-ass circle with a little mini circle of cards inside it, as if you were looking down upon a pony keg stacked on top of a regular keg. Players take turns guessing if the card they pick up out of the outer circle will be red or black. If they're right, they get to make other people drink the following amount:

2–10: Face value
Jack: Four or eleven
Queen: Three or twelve
King: Two or thirteen
Ace: One or fourteen

But, if you pick the wrong card color, then *you* have to drink however many the card is worth. The reason the higher cards are worth odd amounts is to the guesser's benefit; if you guess the wrong color and draw an ace, you only have to drink one, but if you correctly guess the color of a jack, you get to hand out eleven.

Note: When you draw cards, it does not have to be in any order. However, you must use up all the cards in the outside circle before drawing from the inner circle.

All right, big card drawer—just because your turn is over doesn't mean you're banging prostitutes. Keep the card you drew on your turn. This card is "on hold" while Player Two goes. Whether Player Two guesses right or wrong, if his card is the same *suit* as yours, you both have to drink three. When this happens, both your cards are still "on hold" until Player Three goes. If *his* card is also the same suit, you all drink six. If Player Four's card is the same suit, you all drink nine. This keeps going around, adding on three drinks each time until the chain of same-suit cards is broken. Remember, these drinks are all in addition to the ones you already have to drink from a player's correct or incorrect guesses.

If Player Two's card is the same value as yours, meaning you drew a jack on your turn and Player Two also drew a jack on his turn following yours, you both have to drink ten. *If* you happen to get a third same card drew in a row, drink twenty each. Your luck blows ass. If you are playing with two or more decks and the exact same card (suit *and* value) is drawn in a row, both players have to finish their drinks.

The reason this game is different than Circle of Wonderfulness is because, when you finish the outside ring, you get the pleasure of starting the inside ring. On the inside ring, every drink is doubled. Yes, *doubled.* So if you correctly guess an ace, you get to hand out twenty-eight drinks. Also, drawing the same suit as the person before you gets better and better (six drinks, twelve, eighteen, twenty-four, etc.).

Another thing about the inner ring is that, by now, you may be somewhat drunk. This is why there are some rules for you to likely break and drink more. This is why Circle of Betterness does indeed have more Betterness than Circle of Wonderfulness. It also has better grammar.

The first rule is thus: You may never draw a card next to the one the person before you drew. This sounds easy but, trust me, it's not—especially when you're forced to break it when there are only two or three cards left. If you break this simple rule, you drink three.

One more: Every single time you drink, ever, you have to have your left leg raised in the air. It doesn't have to be that high, but if someone catches you with your leg down, you drink three. This game is not for the amateur drinker . . . or parapalegic.

Continuing Education: For more on *The Imbible*'s original series, "The Alcohol Life Cycle," please see Circle of Extreme Happy Greatness below. Bring tissues—it gets emotional.

CIRCLE OF EXTREME HAPPY GREATNESS

The Alcohol Life Cycle—Part 3 of 3: After alcohol reaches maturity, it goes off to work at a grocery store, a bar, or as a bomb ingredient in a black market Liberian illegal arms–trafficking operation. Either way, it will soon retire, and then die—but rest assured: all alcohol goes to heaven. By hungover-puking dormie, front-yard-pissing frat guy, or heavily urinating barfly, alcohol makes its way back to Father Earth, who drinks it down, filters it in his fatherly liver, and pisses it down upon us once again. This is the Alcohol Life Cycle.

Players: Unless you are seriously one of the top twenty drinkers on the planet, you'll need at least ten or fifteen players. If your soul happens to be inhabiting a garbage can, you should be good with five or six.

Supplies:
- At least two decks of cards
- To start sober, would be a good "supply"

Beer: Enough beer to fill one of those water tanks where you throw a baseball at a target and try to dunk your teacher or some wannabe rodeo queen in a white shirt

Warning: This game is not for the amateur drinker, or for people who are somewhat excited about living the full extent of their life.

Objective: To make it around all three circles, ultimately capturing what you will only be able to describe as "Extreme Happy Greatness" moments before you pass-the-fuck-out

Basics: First, lose your sanity. Then, arrange where you'll fit the entertainment system in your brain—you're about to have a lot of extra room with all those annoying cells gone. Lastly, lay out the two or three decks face down in three concentric circles, meaning there is one largest outer ring, a slightly smaller second ring, and a third ring inside the other two, like three diminishing bagels. Players take turns guessing if the card they pick up will be red or black. If they are correct, they get to make whomever they want the following amounts drunker before he passes away:

2–10: Face value
Jack: Four or eleven
Queen: Three or twelve
King: Two or thirteen
Ace: One or fourteen

If you guess the wrong color, you suck, and have to drink the card's worth. But, lucky for you, the higher cards are worth either a lot or a little, so when you guess the wrong color and draw an ace, you only have to drink one, but if you guess the right color and draw an ace, you hand out fourteen. Hooray.

But the card you drew has not yet served its full purpose. You have to hold on to the card you drew as Player Two goes, and if his card is also the same suit as yours, you both have to drink three. If this happens, you *both* hold on to your cards while Player Three goes and drink six if his card is also the same suit. If Player Four's card is the same suit, you all drink nine. Keep going around like this and adding on three drinks until the string of suited cards is broken.

Also, say the card you drew was a five, and Player Two draws a five; you both need to drink ten. It doesn't matter the suit; if the value is the same, you drink ten. If the value *and* suit are the same, you both finish your drinks, and then pour another and keep drinking until your friends are satisfied.

Oh how cruel you are, Circle of Extreme Happy Greatness.

By now you should be feeling wonderfulness, but it's about to get Betterness, and the grammar just keeps getting worse. After the outer ring, you move into the second ring, where everything you ever have to drink—ever—is doubled. *Every drink.* There are also two rules you must follow: (1) you may never draw a card next to the one the person before you drew, with three-drink penalty for breaking it, and (2) every single time you drink—ever—you have to have your left leg raised in the air. It doesn't have to be all that high, but if someone catches you putting it down, drink three. If someone calls you out when you're in compliance, kick them with your already-raised leg.

Now comes the Extreme Happy Greatness and, oh boy, is it extreme. The third ring, the smallest and most inner ring, is where grown men cry and piss themselves. Every drink in the innermost ring is **tripled tripled tripled** . . . sorry; I thought an echo would make it more dramatic. Yes, this means that if you correctly guess a red ace, you can hand out *forty-two* drinks and, yes, if you are playing, you must drink them. No backing down now. This game separates the men from the boys (and the Social Security–collecting from the oh-what-a-sad-early-death people).

If you incorrectly guess a black ten, *you* drink thirty drinks. If you draw the same suit as the person before you, you both drink nine. If it happens again, you drink eighteen, and so on. If the same exact card is drawn in a row in the innermost circle, both players must consume the entire liquid contents of the closest fridge, ketchup and all.

Seriously, though, if the amount of drinks this game asks of you is too much, don't try to prove that you're a badass. There's nothing funny about puking, regardless of what my editor seems to think.

That said, have an Extreme Happy Greatness time!

COPS AND ROBBERS

Other Acceptable Names: NBA Players and Law Enforcement, Drug Lords and Narcotics Unit, Immigrants and Border Police, College Kids and University PD, My Blacked-Out Buddy Paul and Unsuspecting Ducks, Drunken Country Boys and Angry Farmers, Spelling and Dan Quayle, Cheap Vodka and Chasers

Players: At least six. Any more than ten makes it impossible, or hilarious; whichever you want.

Supplies:

- A deck of cards
- A pretty much perfectly circular table
- Geometry skills (for the table's sake)

Beer: The higher the cards you choose, the more beer you'll need (you'll see).

Objective: If you're the robber, get away with "making the deal." If you're the cop, catch the robber before you get blacked out and crash into a metaphorical tree.

Choosing Your Ski Mask: First of all, this game is priceless. Probably should be in the "Classics" section, but whatever. So, get enough cards from the deck so each player has one. However, one of the cards has to be an ace and one a king (and you can only have one of each). The dealer awkwardly shuffles the six or so cards face down, to lose track of where the ace and king are. Remember, the higher the value of the other cards in the mix, the more people will drink. High cards = good.

The dealer is the shortest person at the table (sorry, Frodo). Midget Man passes out one card to each player, including himself. The person who gets the ace is the robber, while the person who gets the king is the cop. If you're the robber, the goal is to wink at somebody and not let anybody else see you do it, especially the cop, not that you know who the cop is. Once you successfully wink at somebody, the winked-at person says aloud, "The deal has been made."

It is now up to the cop to guess who winked at the person. If he guesses somebody and is wrong, that player flips over their card and the cop has to drink that many (two to ten = face value, jack = eleven, queen = twelve). After drinking, he moves on and keeps guessing until he finds the robber, drinking the allotted amount of drinks with each wrong guess. The robber only drinks if the cop catches him on the *first* guess. If the robber is unfortunate enough to wink at the cop, he is obviously busted and has to drink fourteen, because he has the ace.

Basically, once the cards are dealt out, everybody sits in silence staring at each other's eyes like some paranoid old witch on LSD as the robber tries to wink slyly at somebody who he hopes isn't the cop. Just wait until people get drunk and try to "secretly" wink at somebody. If you're one of those freaks who can't wink, you can nod or just blink both eyes rapidly at someone. Good luck, weirdo.

Real-Life Lessons by Alex Bash: If you are an underage college male caught drinking on campus by university police, this is the game they play to see if you are guilty. Seriously. I've evaded many MIPs by not winking at the guy in dark blue with the gun. If you're a female, they play the how-big-are-your-tits-compared-to-your-sluttiness game. I *always* win this one.

CRAZY EIGHTS

Crazy Fuck! Literally. Since we're on the subject of "crazy" things, how the hell did dinosaurs have sex? They'd never be able to stand back up after missionary, and those damn tails block any hopes of doggie-style. Well, some creepy scientist guy actually wrote an entire book on dinosaur sex, and I'd quote him but I don't like bibliographies. Or science. Or the thought of dinosaurs having sex. *Wow,* I need to drink less.

Players: At least three. Five or six will work the best. Two is simply too little, while seven or more is just overwhelming. Alone wouldn't work, and having zero players may cause some complications.

Supplies: A deck of cards

Beer: Eight crazy beers per person. If you don't know what makes a beer crazy, you don't have the nipples to handle it.

Objective: No winners. Just drinks and laughs.

Let's Get Fucking Crazy! Get the four eights out of the deck and lay them face up on the table vertically, as if they're standing on top of one another. Like elephants in a cartoon circus, or *Maxim* models in your adolescent daydreams. Deal out the rest of the cards evenly to everybody else. Players take turns laying down a card next to an eight of the same suit. Even if you can't lay a card right next to the eight, you always play each turn. These eights are balls deep in craziness!!

However many cards there are in the row, including the one you lay down, determines how much somebody is going to drink. If you can't lay a card down directly next to an eight or next to a card that's "touching" an eight, you have to drink however many cards are in that row, including what you lay down. So, if the clubs row had the seven through ten (four cards), and the closest one you have is the queen, you'd lay it down and drink five.

If you *are* able to lay down the card either directly above or below a card that's "touching" an eight, you get to hand out drinks equal to however many cards are in that particular row, plus yours. So in the above example with the row of four clubs, if you had the jack of clubs and laid it down, you'd hand out five drinks. This also works if, say, that previous player *did* lay down the queen, and then the next player laid down the jack of clubs, thus connecting the queen with the other four cards; he'd get to hand out six, because there are now six connected cards in the row.

If any of that sounds confusing, it'll make more sense when you see the cards laid out. It's like taking first-grade math all over again, except this time you're pissing yourself for a whole new socially acceptable reason. Funny how that works.

Oh, and aces are high or low. Or medium. If you figure that one out, e-mail me.

More Crazy Shit! Every game after the first, you have to trade three cards with somebody. For the second game, trade straight across from you; the third game, trade to your left; the fourth, to your right, and so on. Do not negotiate when you're trading; try to pass the person your "worst" three cards, like ones that are nowhere near one another or appear to be covered in old cream cheese.

Crazy Fucking Strategies and Options!!!

- If you rid yourself of a certain suit and try to control one, you'll probably be well off, unless you get passed the king and two of the suit you were trying to get rid of and suffer the consequences, which will probably be thinking it's a good idea to call over your ex-girlfriend *and* current girlfriend. They both like you, right? Right?

- If you want, apply rules to certain cards, like a two is wild, a red jack is worth double the drinks, or a king clears the line. You decide.

Options that Are Completely Fucking Logical!!!

- Sometimes the hands are so well diversified that everyone can always play a card next to another. What you can do to solve this is make it so you have to play cards in a certain order. For example, the first round of turns, everyone has to play a diamond and if someone can't, he drinks five. The second round of turns, everyone has to play a spade and if he can't, he drinks five, and so on.

- Another way to play is to lay down one eight at a time and take turns playing on it until the whole suit is exhausted. Again, if someone can't play a card on his turn, he drinks five. He could also "not play" as a strategy if the current line is long and he can't play next to something.

Top 10 Reasons why Crazy Eights should be played in First Grade: Although it sounds perverse, this game would be very educational for first graders. You doubt me? Checkout my flawlessly copy-and-pasted bullet points and you'll change your mind.

10. Not only would they learn to add and subtract, they'd learn that it's not okay to grab your teacher's ass—while they're still too young for prosecution!
9. What's the worst thing a drunken first grader could do—crash the toy fire truck into the Legos?
8. Talk about creative writing! I just heard little Billy talking about a green fairy named Absinthe! Now tell me that he'd come up with that sober?
7. Let little girls and boys make drunken mistakes before they can get pregnant or acquire STDs.
6. Tired of annoying little shits being hyperactive in the early A.M. hours? Let the hangover take care of that.

5. Little Freddy Fat Cakes will be forced to exercise as he lifts Carly the Cow's heavy legs into the air and pumps the world's first all-Legos keg.
4. Future lawyers of the world will get the chance to practice drinking before the inevitable alcoholism kicks in.
3. Can you get a DUI riding a bike around the playground? I think not!
2. Worried about your son being called a vagina when he can't hold down his alcohol come college? Get 'em started early!
1. Alcohol + jungle gym = crazy fun.

DROWN THE CLOWN

As obvious as it may sound, do not mix wine and gin. If you happen to mix them, do not use the result to play Beer Pong. If you use it to play Beer Pong, do not lose to your roommate. If you lose to your roommate, hide his Sharpies so he can't draw an erect penis on the back of your neck. If you get an erect penis drawn on the back of your neck, notice it before meeting your girlfriend's parents for the first time. Trust me.

Players: Between three and thirteen

Supplies:
- A deck or two of cards
- A garbage bag to use as a condom (have you *seen* the size of those feet?!)

Beer: Enough to drown the clown that haunts your dreams

Where Does the Deep-Seated Fear of Clowns Come From? The fear of clowns comes from being a pussy. Honk honk.

Objective: To yell, "Clown!" before anybody else

Basics: Deal out the cards evenly. Players sit in anticipation as they slowly count to three together and then flip over their top card. If any two, three, or four people have the same card, one of them has to yell, "Clown!" before anybody else who has the same card. The last one to yell has to drink the value of the card (two to ten=face value, jack=eleven, queen=twelve, king=thirteen, ace=fourteen). If you preemptively yell, "Clown," and no one has the same card as you, drink the value of your card. The more people you play with, the harder it gets to see everybody's card quickly.

Beyond the Balloon Animals:

- Instead of yelling, "clown," try yelling something like, "Antidisestablishmentarianism!" or "Horse cock!" or "I'm currently experiencing a painful discharge!"
- If you're super intense, try flipping over two cards each, and yelling different words or phrases for pairs and three- or four-of-a-kind. Drink accordingly.

Drowning Clowns in the Classroom: It's difficult, but made easier if you follow my three easy steps:

1. When pairs arise, choose from the following phrases to shout:
    - "I can't find the derivative!"
    - "Neoliberal industrialists would disagree!"
    - "Page one hundred eighty-three has an informative diagram!"
    - "I would totally hook up with Professor McCarthy!"

2. Text books were made for flasks. No sane person can write nine hundred pages about postcolonialism and not repeat himself. Therefore, simply cut out a flask-size square in pages 350–750 and stick it in. If questioned, you have bad vision and must hold the book up to your face to read. And swallow the information. You're a very dedicated student.

3. Blackmail. If they catch you drinking, you caught them doing coke in the faculty lounge. It's the twenty-first century—facts are irrelevant if you shout loud enough!

DRUNKEN PIRATES

Random Act of Kindness: Next time you're at a drive-through coffee stand, slip the cashier $5 and whisper, "Use this to pay for the next customer's coffee." The next customer will be so pleased that he or she will do the same thing, and it'll continue all day! Hooray for humanity! Hide in a bush and drink five for each satisfied customer. Drink ten for the douche bag who breaks the streak.

Players: Arrg, a pirate be playin' with whoever he likes now, laddie.

Supplies: Cards, me matey. Ay, and bad eggs.

Grog: Arrg, a pirate be drinkin' all yer grog! (Note: "Grog" is water mixed with rum at a 4:1 ratio.)

Objective: To sail up and down ye river of cards and be merry and full of rum. Ravaging and hording is optional.

Basics of Plundering: First off, you scallywags, there be no normal English speakin' on my watch. If ye be caught ye shall be thrown in ye dungeon quarters, ay! With grog, of course, of which you shall pillage two drinks.

Okay, it's way too hard to type like a pirate would, but try to talk like one if you can.

So, deal every player four cards face up in front of them. Keep them there for the remainder of the game. The dealer starts dealing cards face up in a row symbolizing the River of Grog. If the value of the first card matches any of your four cards, you drink one. If you have two of that card, you drink two, and so on. The second card dealt works the same but you drink two for every card you possess. He keeps going on to the third, fourth, fifth, and sixth cards, each time adding one drink per card if you have the same one in front of you.

Then, you start heading back down the river to your pirate headquarters, to file taxes on the plunder you pillaged. Pull a U-turn with the cards, Mr. Dealer. *This* time, however, if a card is laid down and you have it in front of you, you get to *hand out* that many drinks. Hand out one drink for each matching card for the first one, two for the next, three . . . four . . . five, and then six drinks for the sixth and final card. Congratulations! You made it home without getting a PUI (Pirating Under the Influence).

At the end, you divide up the booty by laying down the next five cards from the deck. However many of these cards you all possess together as a crew, you drink together. Hear, hear! A pirate's life for me!

For the Grog-Filled Pirate with Lots of Free Time: Build a plank. Seriously. Even if it's just a two-by-four lying on the ground. Then, whenever somebody has to drink four or more drinks, he'll have to walk the plank. If he falls off the plank and into the treacherous water of your living room floor, his drink amount is doubled. And, just as real pirates would, feel free to pelt him with empty cans of grog along the way.

Glossary, Ho! In the event of a mutiny, the outcome shall be decided by whoever can use the most pirate terms in a sentence and make sense. For example:

> "Handsomely belay, ye Jack Tar—ye shanty is bilge! No quarter and ye'll kiss the gunner's daughter and splice the mainbrace!"
>
> Loose translation:
>
> "Quickly cease and desist, sailor—you are singing nonsense! If you resist, you will be bent over and have drinks forced down your throat!"

DRUNK DRIVER

Warning: If you ever, ever, *ever* drink and drive, I will personally hunt you down and knock you out. And steal your wallet. And your hat, if it fits me.

Warning: Consumption of alcohol may lead you to believe that you have mystical kung fu powers. You are not a ninja. Your name is Chuck Schwartz; you drive a Mazda.

Personal Warning from the Author: Putting a metal desk chair over your head when you pass out on the floor will not protect you from mice named Qualm.

Players: You only really need two, but it's best to have a crowded car to keep you awake and scream when you start drifting.

Supplies:

- A bang-load of cards
- The ability to make car noises

Beer: Enough to keep your BAC under your state's over-twenty-one legal driving limit. Just kidding.

Objective: To make it down the imaginary road without imaginarily crashing

Swerving: The dealer, who we'll say is riding shotgun, lays eight cards face down in the shape of a windy road. If you come from some hick town with no roads, just lay them down in a "line," one of those straight things, like a trough of pig slop or row of corn.

Choose someone to be the driver; everybody drinks when the driver does because, as we all know, felons stick together! The driver starts turning over cards from the parking lot (first card) and keeps going until he arrives back in his driveway (last card). If the overturned card is a two through a ten, nothing happens and you move on to the next card. If the card is a jack, the driver and his passengers drink one and lay one more card face down to the end of the road. If it is a queen, they all drink two and you add two cards; for a king, you drink three and add three; and for an ace, you drink four and add four.

You made it home DUI-free when you flip over the last card. Make sure to make loud car noises as you drive, and skidding or crashing noises when you hit a face card. The longer the road, the rougher the drive, in case you couldn't figure that out on your own. If you aren't getting drunk enough, have someone's hat fly out the window and turn around to get it or "pop a tire" and double all the drinks.

Important: I cannot stress how important car noises are. The game should almost be called Car Noises and Lame Drunken Car Jokes.

Oh, and by the way: you never only have five gears.

Drunks of Hazard:

- Build ramps out of flattened twenty-four-cases, trees out of empty bottles, rivers of spilled beer, and mud out of six-pack rings. Extra drinks apply for hitting face cards on these obstacles.
- Maybe, and I just thought of this, have a second car start behind you on a second road when you get one-third of the way along, and have them be the cop! Take turns flipping cards and have the cop car drink and lay out more cards when it hits a card valued two through five.
- Two words: Hot Wheels.

DRUNKER DRIVER

Warning: If you ever in your life drive drunk, I will take the liberty of stealing your car, selling it for parts, and using the money to buy you a hooker so you can get gonorrhea and learn a fucking lesson. Don't . . . drive . . . drunk!

Personal Warning from the Author: Consumption of alcohol may lead you to capture a duck and lock it in a room with a previously passed-out Duncan.

Personal Advice from the Author: Tape the windows shut first. Quack quack.

Players: Bare minimum is two (one for each car), but we all know it's easier to avoid a cop that's chasing you by having passengers pee onto its windshield.

Supplies:

- A deck of cards
- Guessing skills
- The lack thereof ability to say, "I've had enough"

Beer: I take no responsibility for the absurd amounts of beer you consume during this game, but will testify at your hearing about how awesome you are for killing a thirty-bomb by yourself. And by "testify" I mean "speak" and by "hearing" I mean "funeral."

Objective: For you and your passengers to make it off the road safely and onto the couch.

Concentrating on the Road: Choose who is going to be the Lead Car and who is going to be the Following Car. Either car can be full of however many guys you want. They fit over thirty midgets in a Volkswagen Bug, didn't they?

Important: Make car noises like it's your job.

Somebody lay down between six and twelve cards in a curvy row (a drunk person's straight line). The more cards, the harder and longer the road. The Lead Car, whether he's alone or with buddies, turns over the first card in the line. As opposed to regular Drunk Driver, the value of the card matters not. The first card is a gimme, but for every other card the Lead Car must guess whether it will be higher or lower than the previous one.

If they are correct in their guess, the Following Car must drink the difference between the first and second card. For example: if the first card was a seven, the Lead Car guessed higher, and the next card was a queen, each passenger in the Following Car would consume five drinks (for the seven, then the eight through queen). Every person has to drink the full amount; it's not five drinks spilt between them.

Value of cards: 2–10 = face value, jack = 11, queen = 12, king = 13, and ace = 14.

If the Lead Car guesses wrong, *they* have to drink the difference between the first and second card. So, if the first card was a seven, like before, and they guessed higher and it turned out to be a three, each passenger in the Lead Car would drink four.

Important: Make car noises like it's your job.

Here's why Drunker Driver is drunker than regular Drunk Driver. If the Lead Car guesses wrong they must move back three spaces, or back to the beginning if they've only moved ahead one or two cards. You also lay cards face down to cover the ones they had to move back across. This may sound harsh, especially if you suck at guessing and can't make it three spaces out of the parking lot, but this is why it's Drunk*er* Driver. Also, the game should last for a while and be fun, not just be some mundane task to be completed before moving on.

Let's be sensitive here—Drunker Driver has feelings, too.

Tips, Hints, and Ideas to Make Your Night More Loud and Obnoxious:

- If you don't like the first card being a gimme, make it so the Lead Car has to guess whether it's red or black before moving on. Also, make this an option for the whole game: if the card is a seven or eight—right in the middle—they can guess fifty/fifty for red or black.

- The Following Car generally just sits back and drinks when the Lead Car messes up but, if that's too boring, have them wager whether the Lead Car will correctly guess the next card or two, and award yourself drinks or pee breaks.

- If you are indeed a badass guesser and drinker, play it this way: If the Lead Car ever guesses wrong, no matter where you are along the road, you start again. Oh, and the number you'll want to have ready to dial is 911.

- If you live in Seattle or some other city with too many people and approximately thirteen combined feet of water-locked road, name each card that makes you drink a different street name that's known for having heavy traffic, such as "Any road to ever exist in the greater Seattle area."

Arriving Safely: Your destination is the beer store. Celebrate with a six-pack, several middle fingers at the cars around you, and a few lengthy honks of the horn.

Important: make car noises like it's your job.

FUCK THE DEALER

Alex's Life Lesson: You'll probably only use 10 percent of the information taught to you throughout your entire schooling career, so why waste precious brain space with things like atomic numbers and calculus and why Indians are always complaining about land rights? See, the reason you feel so smart when drinking is because the brain cells containing worthless shit are sacrificing themselves for the important things, like location of clit and stock market lingo. The more you drink, the more you'll be able to focus on what really matters, like sex, intercourse, fucking, making love, screwing, and fornicating.

Players: Works best with five or six.

Supplies:
- A deck of cards
- Mathematic reasoning skills/lack of mathematic reasoning skills

Beer: If you're at the beach, get Corona. Damn marketing . . .

Objective: To guess the card the dealer is holding and not get too drunk to forget to wrap it up

Lubing Up: Anybody can start as dealer. Starting can either be very bad or very good, but you won't know until you're playing, so just volunteer and then get a fake emergency phone call if it starts looking glum.

It's everyone versus the dealer. The dealer has the full deck of cards and looks at the top one. Player One tries to guess what the card is. If he gets it right, the dealer drinks ten. This is called "fucking the dealer" and is very hard to do, mainly because he still has pants on. If he guesses wrong (which he usually will), the dealer tells him if the card is higher or lower than his first guess, and Player One has one more chance to guess. If he gets it right, the dealer drinks five. This is called "tickling the dealer's balls" and is difficult but doable if you really finger the crotchal area. If he gets it wrong, he has to drink however many cards he is away from what the card really is.

For example, the dealer looks at the card—it's a three. Suit doesn't matter. Player One guesses, "Jack." Dealer says, "Lower." Player One guesses, "Eight." Dealer laughs in his face and turns it over. Since eight is five numbers away from three, Player One drinks five drinks.

Regardless of what Player One does, it is now Player Two's turn, and he does the same thing with guessing and drinking. The dealer gets to pass the deck along to the next person when he has gone through every person playing *in a row* without anyone's guessing a correct card. So if you're the dealer and are playing with three other people, and all three of them can't correctly guess their card on the first or second guess, you get to pass on the deck.

However, the dealer has to get through everyone *in a row* before passing it on. Meaning, if he's playing with six others and gets through Players One, Two, Three, Four, and Five, but then Player Six guesses right, the dealer has to go back through

Players One, Two, Three, Four, Five, and then Six again before being relieved of duty. Mirrors come in handy.

Whether Player One guesses right or wrong, the dealer then lays the card face up on the table and will eventually make a clock with all the cards, putting the twos on the top right in the "one o'clock position" and going around two, three, . . . all the way to the "twelve o'clock" position with the aces. As players guess cards right and wrong, it will begin to help them determine the odds of what the card could be.

Near the end of the game, almost all the cards will be laid out so it will be much easier for players to guess correctly. This is why being dealer first can be bad if the deck gets back around to you, and why you should have a solid plan of escape, like being able to push your body into anaphylactic shock. If there are only threes, tens, and kings left, the players can guess ten on the first guess and get it on the second guess every time. If the deal never gets back around to you because you're playing with too many people or everybody sucks at guessing, then great. If it *does* get back to you, then, well, guess what, Mr. Dealer—you've been fucked.

FUCK YOUR NEIGHBOR

Caution: *Explicit Fucking Language.*
The many uses for the word *fuck*:

Greetings:	"How the fuck are you?"
Dismay:	"Fuck it."
Fraud:	"I got fucked."
Lost:	"Where the fuck are we?"
Pain:	"Fuck!"

Pissed off: "Fuck!"
Panic: "Fuck!"
Apathy: "Fuck it."
Dismissal: "Go play hide-and-go-fuck-yourself."
Love: "Fuck you."
Approval: "Fan-fucking-tastic!"
Sign Language: "_____"
Politics: "I Fucked Iowa's Caucus."

Players: Try fifty-two. If not, five to ten will work.

Supplies:
- No sympathy
- No mercy
- No cards. Just kidding; you need cards.

Beer: However many it will take you to want to fuck your neighbor . . . in the card game. That's right: two whole beers.

Objective: To end up with the highest card or, if not, then just not the lowest card.

Going Next Door: Take turns being the dealer, going clockwise. The dealer deals out one card per person face down, each player looking at his own card. Keep in mind you want the highest card possible at the end of the game (two is low, ace is high). The person to the left of the dealer is Player One and goes first, choosing whether he wants to keep his card or trade it with the person to his left, Player Two. If Player One chooses to trade, Player Two must abide, but once the trade is done, Player One cannot take it back. So if he traded and got a lower card, too bad for him. If he chooses to keep his initial card, the turn moves on to Player Two who has the same options Player One had.

This goes around the table until it gets back to the dealer, who has the choice to either trade with Player One or to keep his initial card. After he is done, everybody flips over their cards, the player with the lowest card drinks five, and the player with the highest card gets to hand out five.

Sneaking out the Window:

- For the second and third games, if you have the right number of players, try trading across the table, or to the right, or even trade once across and *then* trade to your left or right. It's neighbor-fucking crazy!
- Maybe throw in the option of drawing from the deck so you could pass, trade, or draw. The possibilities are endless! (Note: Possibilities not actually endless.)
- Maybe do it where each player gets three cards and can trade one, two, or three cards to try to make pairs, three-of-a-kind, etc. Or just play poker.

Back Through the Window:

- Keep in mind, if you are the dealer, you should pay close attention to whether Player One chooses to pass, because it means he has a high enough card to not want to trade. Eventually, it'll be your turn to trade with him.
- Player One, keep in mind that the dealer is watching you, so maybe pull a little reversal and keep your really low card in hopes that (a) Player Two doesn't have a really high card that you could have traded for, and (b) the dealer's card is low enough that he indeed does want to see what you have.

Hiding the Evidence: Poker faces are good, but what about that shit-faced guy who just quotes dumb movies and makes unacceptable comments about women's suffrage and socioeconomic inequality? What the hell card does he have?!

GHRF (GET HAMMERED REALLY FAST)

Traffic Explained: Traffic, one of life's most irritating fucking mysteries, can be explained by a night of drinking. See, you start the night (get on the road) and cruise through four or five beers (a few miles) with just a buddy or two (a few cars). Then, more people (other cars) start coming over from other houses (entry ramps). Although there is plenty of room at the party (freeway), the added guests make it harder to stumble around at your leisure (full speed) because you never know when they may stumble backward (brake suddenly, change lanes) and cause an accident (spilled drink). Always, avoid cops (cops).

Players: Four works best

Supplies:
- A parched throat
- Cards
- A shot glass

Beer: A little beer, a little hard A, a little unmarked-bottle-from-granny's-liquor-cabinet; we don't discriminate.

Note: GHRF is not just a simple game to get you tanked quickly before an event that is enhanced by intoxication (baseball game, movie, exam, funeral, political sex scandal, etc.). It's also a devious ploy disguised by a vague acronym. You can trick Trying-to-not-get-too-drunk-tonight Guy by saying, "Dude, it's just GHRF, you'll be fine."

Objective: Get Hammered Really Fast And Start All Words With A Capital Letter!!! GHRFASAWWACL!!!

GH: Get the jacks, queens, kings, and aces out of the deck for your use; we won't be needing those measly lower cards. Fill the shot glass with hard alcohol. Put all the selected cards face down in a messy pile and take turns drawing one, going clockwise. Here's what the cards mean:

Ace: You drink 5.
King: Tell someone else to drink five.
Queen: Social, everybody drinks five.
Jack: Play a word association game.

The player who drew the jack starts by saying a word—any word. Everybody then goes in a circle, saying a word that is associated with the chosen word. It doesn't have to be a synonym or even in the same category, it just has to be associated with it.

You'll all have to be judges as to whether a word counts. If you think it doesn't, give the person who said it ten seconds to explain himself. If you vote that his word wasn't associated enough, he takes the shot. Also, if someone takes too long or repeats somebody else's word, he takes the shot.

Word association example: baseball, peanuts, Yankees, home run, Babe Ruth, Hank Aaron, triple play, money . . . ummmm, no. A player may have said, "Money," because MLB players are paid a lot, but it's a stretch because you can say, "Money," with association to almost anything. Drink, bitch! GHRF!!

Some of the fun is trying to convince your buddies that "the falcon mating cycle" is of course associated with "sex positions." Just tell them it's European.

A Little Something for the Reader: If you are reading aloud to anticipating GHRFers or just browsing through, please ask yourself the following question and abide by the punishment:

Question: What is *acronym* an acronym for?

Think about it . . .
Think about it . . .

Think about it . . .
Think about it . . . Done!

Example Answers: Annoyingly Cryptic References of Names You Memorize, Abbreviations Cropping Random Objects Numbing Your Mind, Alcoholic Crayons Ramming Orbs Near Your Mother, or Alex's Corny Ripoffs of Nothing You Manifest.

Punishment: Drink five for every minute it took you to come up with a clever answer.

GIVE OR TAKE

Why should we be allowed to drink alcohol in class?

1. We learn better when we're relaxed.
2. Opening up class discussion will no longer be thirty seconds of, "Anyone . . . anyone?"
3. Really want participating volunteers? You got 'em! Put me on stage, bitch!
4. We learn best in our natural environment.
5. Professors—looking for that midlife crisis act of infidelity? *Waaaay* easier.

Players: Three to seven homies to get crunked out . . . fo sho

Supplies: Cards

Beer: Use whatever alcoholic beverage you like. Be creative. Like, instead of Bud Light, get Miller Lite! Whoa! Slow down, champ!

Official Shouldn't-Be-Famous Saying of Give or Take: "Some days chicken, some days feathers."

Objective: To get lucky and hand out drinks. It's *very* complicated.

Giving to Take, Taking to Give . . . or Something like That: Deal everybody four cards face up in front of them. The dealer is then going to deal the top card off the remaining deck face up on the table, but first all players have to declare if they're going to "give" or "take." You must always alternate "giving" drinks and "taking" drinks, unless you declare "take" twice in a row, in which case you can then "give" twice in a row. First, let's look at some sample hands:

TheHamster:	10, 6, jack, 10
TwoHole:	2, 3, ace, king
ShitBag:	5, 7, queen, 9
Walnut:	5, 3, 4, 10

Let's say all the players declare they are going to "give" their first drinks, and the card that comes up is a three. Walnut and TwoHole get to give out one drink each to whomever they want because they have a three in their hand. Next, they all declare "take" because they are choosing to alternate for now and it makes explaining a hell of a lot easier.

The second card the dealer turns over is worth two drinks for each one you have in your hand. Let's say the next card is a ten; TheHamster drinks four and Walnut drinks two. If TheHamster had chosen "take" in the first round and "give" in the second round, then he'd be giving away four drinks.

For the third card dealt, you give or take three drinks for each matching card you have; for the fourth card, you give or take four drinks; and for the fifth and final card, you give or take five drinks. After the fifth card, you start going back down. The sixth card is worth four drinks, the seventh is worth three, the eighth is worth two, and the ninth is worth one drink just like the first card. The tenth and final card laid down is worth ten drinks but you can only choose to "give" them if you make the seventh, eighth, and ninth cards all "takes." This way it's a gamble, 'cause if you don't have the tenth card, you wasted cards seven, eight, and nine.

This is the end of the first game. You're all winners in Give or Take! Now, go get some chicken! Or feathers! Or whatever!

Feather Plucking:

- If you want to have winners or losers, get a piece of paper and something to write with, and give a point to a player each time he successfully gets to hand out a drink, in respect to his lucky guesses.

- If you're hard core, you could make each round longer by playing cards until they are worth eight or ten drinks per matching card and *then* going back down.

Grilling the Chicken:

- Try it with two decks of cards shuffled together and deal each player six cards to start with. It starts getting sloppy (read: picture worthy) when somebody is dealt four kings and a fifth comes on the tenth card.

- For any of you odd people who don't like to gamble but like to drink, you can justify playing this game by being somebody's "Operational Pragmatics Consultant" and simply instructing him on the advantages and disadvantages of giving or taking. But like all good OPCs, when your boss drinks, you drink. That's how it works, right?

GO FISH

Don't you just love how a simple children's game turns into a drinking game? But maybe it says something about us as humans, that we're all kids at heart. We still yearn for the simplicities of youth, the freedom and aspirations, the unresponsibilitilessness, and the ability to make up words. We also realize that playing with Legos would be *waaaay* more fun when you're hammered. And you thought Barbie was hot while you're sober . . .

Players: Between two and five

Supplies:

- A deck of cards
- A decent memory
- See-through vision

Beer: Two for each fish bowl you filled with beer in hopes of getting your fish drunk. Two more for each time you had to flush the toilet.

Objective: To end up with the most pairs at the end

Casting Out: Deal seven cards to each player. You may need two decks if playing with hella (eight) or more people. Lay down any pairs you are dealt to begin with, you lucky bastard. Players take turns going clockwise around the circle, asking somebody if that person has a card in his hand to match a lonely card in the player's hand. If the player you asked has the card, he gives it to you and you lay down that pair and get to ask again.

I can't believe I'm explaining how to play Go Fish.

You keep asking until someone doesn't have a matching card for yours. When this happens, he says, "Go fish," and you draw the top card from the remaining deck. If the card you draw is the card you just asked for, lay the pair down and keep going with your turn. If the card you draw completes another pair you asked for on a previous turn or one you haven't asked for yet, you lay the pair down but do not get to go again. The game keeps going around in circles until eventually one person pairs up his last remaining card. All the players count the pairs in front of them, usually adding two or three because no one will notice, and the person with the most is declared the winner.

Important: When you drink,

- Every time you have to give away a card to somebody who guesses it, drink two.
- Every time you draw a card that completes any pair in your hand, drink two.
- For every pair you got dealt in the beginning, drink two.
- Every time you have to "go fish," drink two.
- For each card you have left in your hand at the end of the game, drink two.
- If you win, hand out five drinks to any one person.
- If you have the least amount of pairs, drink five.
- For every four-of-a-kind you have laid down (two pairs of the same card), hand out four.

Getting Fishy: Optional: Try having to say a different animal name every time you would say, "Go *fish.*" This may sound easy as hell but, trust me, after the usual dog, cat, bear, and so forth, it gets hard. If someone takes too long to pick an animal or repeats one, he drinks two.

P.S. There is only one kind of Barbie, and that is Anatomically Impossible Barbie. The best one ever.

GOLF

Once a sport for older gentlemen, this is now a card game for younger dudes whose idea of a three wood is how erect you can get after eight beers.

Players: Between three and six will do just fine, assuming you have a full bag of clubs

Supplies: Golf balls (cards)

Beers: One for each hole (eighteen)

Rearrange the letters to form the name of a famous golfer: LACK SUCK JAIN

Objective: Like in real golf, to get the lowest score and biggest Nike contract

Teeing Off: Deal everybody four cards face down in a line. Each player can only look at his two outside cards. You want to make your four cards equal the lowest total amount. Here's how cards are valued:

Jack:	0 points
Five:	0 points
Ace:	1 point
2–10:	face value
Queen:	12 points
King:	13 points

This game is sometimes called Jacks and Fives or the Jackson Five, due to the zero point value of jacks and fives. The player to the left of the dealer goes first by drawing a card off the top of the deck and either replacing one of his cards with it or discarding it face up in a pile next to the deck. Then Player Two can either draw from the top of the deck or pick up the card Player One discarded. You may never pick up a card that has a card on top of it; it's buried forever, like Atlantis . . . and Sir Winston Churchill.

Generally, you replace your two outside cards that you've looked at first. When you are satisfied with them, you should replace your two middle cards that you haven't seen yet. This is risky, because the first time you see them will be in the discard pile, which can be very disheartening as you discard a jack, five, or ace, and watch Player Two pick it up on his turn with a grin. Then again, you can breathe a sigh of relief as you toss away kings and queens.

Once you think you have the best hand, you knock in place of your turn. When you knock, you don't pick up or discard a card. Each player then has one more turn and, when it gets back to you, everybody turns his cards over, revealing the winner and losers. The person with the lowest hand is the winner, and automatically gets to hand out five drinks. All other players have to drink the difference between the winner's hand and theirs. For example, if the winner got a total hand value of 3 (two jacks, an ace, and a two) and you got a total hand value of 6, you would drink three. If your hand totalled 10, you'd drink seven, and so on.

For Businessmen who Love Booze but Hate Golf: One of the supposed perks of corporate America is getting to play golf on the clock with "the boss." Many young men are (at least I think) brainwashed into liking golf because they think it's "what you do when you're a guy." And that's fine, but for the few of us who'd rather watch YouTube videos and drink one for each video that could be used as blackmail, there is a simple way to make golf enjoyable.

Drinking with *Actual* Golf: Before starting the game, make sure you all sign a contract stating that the scores you shoot will never be counted in sober golf disputes. That is, unless you're like me and do everything better when drunk, like basketball, Ping-Pong, and contract killing. What you do is, when playing a real course, choose the "par" of each hole, usually one or two beers. For each beer you drink above "par," you get one under par. So, if you decide that the first hole is a "par 2" and you drink three beers before teeing off on the second hole, you get a birdie. If you drink four beers, you get an eagle, and so on. For eighteen-hole courses, use teams.

Note: I'm not sure how DUI laws work with golf carts, but if it's fine, then ooooooh boy! Bumper carts it is!

HORSE RACES

Drinking Translations:

"I'm totally fine to drive home."—"I'm wasted but don't want anybody to see I'm going home with my ex."

"I've already had, like, ten beers!"—"I've only had two drinks but need an excuse to act this way."

"Ever tried a Body-Shot?"—"I'm willing to tongue tequila if it means getting to lick you."

Players: Seriously, ten or twenty works the best, but you really only need four.

Supplies:
- A loud and hopefully drunk and participating audience
- A deck of cards
- The ability to make up funny/disgusting names to yell during the race

Beer: You drink your bet. The more balls you have, the more beer you'll need.

Legend Has It: The louder you yell and cheer for your horse, the faster it goes. In horse racing, *the cards come alive . . .* (cue creepy music).

Objective: For your horse to win! Go, Labia!

Horsing Around: Get the four aces out of the deck and line them up as if they were horses ready to race. You can even build little gates around them with pretzels or peanuts, if you are so inclined. Line up six face-down cards on either side of the horses, symbolizing the outside of the racetrack. It should look like a big horseshoe made of cards.

This used to be optional, but I've made it mandatory: You have to name your horse, and it can't be something normal. Choose a category like reproductive organs or fake mixed drinks to name your horse, and yell and scream the name as your horse advances down the track.

Before starting the game, everyone picks which horse to bet on, bet a certain number of drinks, and then drink the bet. If you win, you get to hand out double this amount; if you lose, you have to drink your initial bet *again*, as well as whatever the winner hands you.

Have someone who is either not playing or too drunk to cheat

be the guy who shuffles the deck after the aces and six cards on each side have been laid down. Now, let the races begin! The dealer lays face up a card from the remaining deck. Whatever suit that card is, the same-suited ace moves forward one space. Usually the dealer also acts as the horse-mover, but anybody can do it as long as everybody is watching.

The dealer deals a second card, and moves the horses accordingly. Everybody is yelling and cheering his respective horse's name wildly, praying for a victory as the fillies advance surprisingly slowly down the imaginary raceway. The first horse to cross the finish line (meaning to clear the last of the six cards on the side) is the winner. Hand out double your previously bet drinks, brave jockey.

But wait, there's more!

Turn over the face-down cards on the side. If any cards bear the suit of the winning horse, those are added to the amount the winner gives out. So, if there is an eight and a six of the winner's suit in the side-rails, he gets to hand out double his initial bet plus fourteen more drinks. This sounds like a lot, but think as if fifteen people are playing and he splits them up. However, he will probably give them all to one person, because you're going to need somebody drunk enough to convince that the hotel manager is at the door so they'll race around and clean up all the beer cans.

Let somebody else shuffle the next game. Make sure to rename all the horses save the winner's (he must hold true to his winning steed). Feel free to change suits if your fucking horse lost. Darn it, Elongated Chode, you let me down again!

Horse Play:

- The reason you can only do six cards on each side is, if you use more, you risk not having one card of a certain suit left in the deck. This is unfair. But, if you don't care about being fair like most of us, feel free to use a longer racetrack.
- Using three or four or fifteen decks for long, intense games is totally fine, even encouraged. May I suggest, however, that if the matching ace comes up, it counts as two spaces? Please?

- Starting a night of drinking with this game may not be the best idea, because the most fun part is the exciting race and the yelling and cheering, which is obviously waaaay better when under the influence.
- A great game to play at home, Horse Races is even more fun to play at the track. Just watch out for the real horses racing around. Man, are they annoying!

ICED HOCKEY

Life Is like a Twelve-Pack: You start out with so much opportunity—anything is possible. You could end up anywhere, like Prague, or New York, or the urinal at Earl's. You can be anything you want: an architect, a musician, or a DUI. By midlife (six beers left), you start to realize what's really important, like family, friends, and scoring big with the chest-friendly bartender. Near the end of life (ten beers deep), you kinda start to go crazy and forget things. And finally, when that last beer is drunk, you'll wake up in a better place (the big sorority in the sky).

Players: Four. Or any number that can be split into even teams, like 6.75.

Supplies:
- Cards
- A hockey puck. Just kidding. Unless it's been injected with liquor.

Beer: Actually, come to think of it, not that much; drink on the side.

Objective: To lay down the same card as the person before you. Yes, like poker's sloppy seconds.

High Sticking: Two teams of two sit around a table. Players on the same team sit across from each other so that they go every other turn. Deal out all the cards evenly, face down; everybody may look at his respective hand. The game moves clockwise, with each player in turn laying a card face up in the center of the table.

Important: There is no conversing with your teammate at all, especially as to what cards you have. There *is* however, hand motions allowed, but each turn can be no more than five seconds long. Make sure you regulate this and fine five drinks per person for excessively long turns. Also, fine people drinks for ridiculously stupid attempts at nonverbal communication. Don't point to yourself to try to describe "king." Only I can do that.

The game is very simple; if Player One on Team A lays down a six, Player One on Team B may score a point if he lays a six on top of it, right afterward. You may *not* play more than one of the same card at a time, at least in the normal version of the game (read below). However, Player Two on Team A (the third person to play) may score 2 points if he also lays down a six after Player One on Team B does. I'm sorry if that sounds confusing, especially if you're already drunk.

Basically, you all just sit around in silence wildly flapping your arms around like drunken idiots, taking turns laying down one card at a time, trying to play the same one as the person before you, thus scoring a point. Also, in case this wasn't clear, the person before you is on the opposite team. If you have more than two players on each team, they always have to be seated alternately around the table like Team A, Team B, Team A, Team B, and so on. Keep track of your points on a piece of paper on the side. The game ends when the final card is played and all hands are empty, save beers.

Losers: however many you lose by, triple that number, and drink it.

Clearing the Puck:

- The reason you can't talk is so you can't communicate what the other team may have in their hands based on what you and your teammate(s) have. Besides, if you knew, then they'd know what not to lay down, so it'd be pointless.
- If you want to play a slightly different way, you can play so that you *can* talk as much as you want but can't ever show each other your cards. The reason why this isn't all that great is if you tell your teammate something about your hand, the other team will know it, too. This is where lies and winking can come in handy. Be clever with this . . .

Sudden Death? After writing this game, I realized there is absolutely no reason why the game is called Iced Hockey. If this bothers you, I suggest frequent and unannounced checking.

INDIAN POKER

5 Reasons Beer Should Be Served at Work:

1. Is an incentive to show up
2. Reduces stress
3. Leads to more honest communications
4. Makes cafeteria food taste better
5. Increases the chance of seeing your boss naked

Players: A couple* works best.

Supplies:

- Cards.
- To feel morally sound about bullying your close friends.

Booze: Absinthe

Objective: Never stray from your Indian names and win the poker hand

Building the Tepee:

First off, give a stereotypical Indian name to the person on your right. If you already have one because you're straight from the tribe, good for you. If not, think of something embarrassing the person did to name him by, such as Chief Pissed Himself or Sergeant, I Saw My Father Doing Illegal Things with the Dog and Was Scarred for Life.

Now deal two cards, face down, to each player. *Do not look at your cards*; just pick them up and put them on your forehead so everybody else can see them, but you can't. Everybody can now see everybody's cards except for his own. All the players can all see *your* card, but you cannot. If you asked me if you could see your own card, I would say no. I *would* tell you, however, that you can see everybody else's cards. The amount of your card that you should personally be able to see is 0 percent, while your vision of others' should be 100 percent. Got it? Good.

The game is played like Texas Hold 'em, which I will explain now for those who don't know how to play.

You make an initial round of betting drinks when you're dealt your first two cards. If you fold because you see everybody else has good hands and you're scared that yours sucks, then (a) you're a pussy, and (b) you are out of this round and don't have to drink unless you are ashamed of yourself, which you should be.

---

* Between three and six.

The bets made by everyone who stays in are put into the "pot," which is the collective amount of drinks that must be drunk by the losers. If somebody bets three, and all four other players call his bet, there are still just three drinks in the pot. There are not three drinks for each person who called, just a collective amount that each person must drink individually at the end.

After you've all bet and folded and whatnot, three cards are laid face up in the middle of the table. These cards can be used by anybody to make his best hand possible; they are "community cards" and are called the "flop."

After another round of betting takes place with these new cards in mind, the dealer lays a fourth card face up on the table, which can again be used by anybody. There are now six possible cards for everybody to choose from, but you may only use five for your final hand, which you will not know until the end, when you all lay 'em down because you can't see two of your own cards (on your head, in case you forgot). After yet another round of betting, a fifth and final community card is laid down. Then there is one final round of betting before everyone lays his cards down to see who won.

Everybody except the winner and those who folded earlier drinks the entire amount of the pot. If you folded earlier, you drink whatever was in the pot at the time you folded.

Float like Butterfly, Sting like Pepper Spray:

- Keep in mind that you'll be betting five times if you stay in until the end, so three or four drinks may not sound like that much at first, but they add up.

- You should obviously try to strong-arm the person with the best unknown hand, by betting a lot of drinks and acting as if his hand is weak and not paying much attention to him, but he could also see through this and realize his hand is kick-ass and double you up on drinks.

- Don't be "That Guy" who always stays in no matter what, just to be tough, or, conversely, just folds at the first sight of a good hand. Be as reasonable as you can while still getting trashed, or it's not as fun. We're all about fun here in *The Imbible.*

- For you poker novices, here is the order of five-card poker hands, from best to worst:

Five of a kind:	You cheated.
Royal flush:	Ten, jack, queen, king, and ace of the same suit
Straight flush:	Any five cards in a row of the same suit
Four of a kind:	Four of the same card
Full house:	Three of the same card, two of another
Flush:	Five cards of the same suit
Straight:	Five cards in a row; suit doesn't matter
Three of a kind:	Three of the same card
Two pair:	Two pairs of cards.
Pair:	Two of the same card, the other three are random.
High card:	If you have none of the above, your highest card is the best you've got (e.g., "Ace High").

INSIDE OUT

Verbal Revolution: There is a revolution coming, and it starts here with *The Imbible*. What revolution, you ask? The Flogging Revolution. For far too long, the word *flog* has been absent from the everyday American vocab. It has been replaced with *abuse* and *assault* and *beat the crap out of.* No more! Flogging must return! I have a dream . . . that one day . . . people of all nations . . . of every language and color . . . can join together as one . . . and flog the shit out of someone. I have a dream, today!

Players: As many as your flogged heart desires

Supplies:
- Cards
- Flogging stick (you *always* flog with a stick)

Beer: Something foreign. Might as well, right?

Definition: (to) Flog—beat with a whip, stick, etc., "as punishment."

Objective: To guess whether the next card laid down will be inside, outside, or equal to the two cards already laid out

A Simple Flog:

Lay two cards face up with space in between for one more. Everybody, at the same time, has to guess whether the next card will be inside or outside the two cards. There doesn't need to be consensus.

Lay the next card from the deck face up between the two already down. If you guessed correctly as to where the card was going to land, hand out three drinks to anybody. If you guessed wrong, drink five. You can also guess "even," which means you think it will be the same as one of the two cards already down. If you get it right, you hand out seven; if you get it wrong, you drink seven. Who's got testicles? Huh?

If you want, you can try to guess exactly what card it will be inside or outside the two cards already down. So you could say "Outside, it's gonna be a six." If you guess half-right, that it'll be outside but not the right card, you drink three and hand out three. If you get both wrong, you drink ten; if you get both right, you hand out fifteen. This is to encourage daring guesses. How about them testes?

If you want to guess the exact card, meaning value *and* suit, you drink twenty if you get it wrong, and hand out twenty if you get it right. Doing this means you have three nuts, which isn't necessarily a good thing.

Outside In: If trying to get at one of your friends for shaving off your eyebrow, telling your parents that there is no such place as Keystone College, or are just a generally mean and prankful person, know this—*Inside Out* is the absolute easiest game in which to stack the deck. Make sure to act surprised when, after laying down a two and king, an ace pops up. For the second time.

Setting Things Straight: Many people are under the impression that if you go over the bar while swinging on a playground, your skin will turn inside out. I happen to have been witness to such an occasion, when a daring soul ventured over the bar. His name was Ryan. He broke his back.

MUSHROOM CLOUD

Female Mushroom: "You know why I like you so much, Male Mushroom?"
Male Mushroom: "No, Female Mushroom, why?"
Female Mushroom: "Because you're a fun guy! Get it?! Ha ha!"
Male Mushroom: "__________"
Male Mushroom: "If you weren't so hot, I'd be fucking Female Shrubbery."

Players: Two or more. Best with five or so.

Supplies:
- Balance
- Cards
- A hydrogen bomb

Beer:

- At least a few unopened ones
- Lots of open ones, also

Objective: To guess the right color and then balance it on the beer

Dropping the Bomb: Set an unopened can of beer in the middle of the table and take turns going clockwise. In turn, each player must guess the color of the top card of the face-down deck sitting next to the unopened beer. If they guess right, they get to hand out as many drinks as the card is worth (two to ten = face value, jack = eleven, queen = twelve, king = thirteen, ace = fourteen). If they guess wrong, they have to drink the number of drinks the card is worth.

Then, no matter how they guessed, they have to set the card on top of the unopened beer can *with 2 of the card's corners hanging off the edge*. Each player does this on his turn and whoever knocks the pile off has to shotgun or chug the beer on which the cards were so perfectly balanced, until Mr. "I-have-no-opposable-thumbs-because-I-threw-gas-on-the-fire" Clumsy had to go and knock them off.

Oh yeah, and each additional card balanced on top must have two corners hanging off the *previous card* as well; you can't just stack a new card in the same place as the one before it with two corners hanging off where the can *should* be. The cards and beer should create a mushroom shape.

If you live in a moist area, try using an actual mushroom from the yard to balance the cards. When someone knocks the cards off, have him eat it.

QUEENS

Ladies: For any women (pronounced: wimin) who think you don't have a fair chance against men in the job market, just remind yourself of your superiority in the marketplace of chess pieces. The queen is by far the most powerful piece on the board, able to move anywhere she wants by simply flashing her tits and strolling on by. I'm kidding, relax—the king is still king no matter how many pawns the queen runs over.

Players: A bunch minus a couple = a few.

Supplies:

- Cards
- Female reproductive organs (a little obvious, but worth a reminder)

Alcohol: Some nice light wine coolers, maybe some mixed drinks

Objective: To get so incredibly drunk that you wear mismatching color schemes! Fashion disaster!

Getting Ready: Lay out the whole deck of cards face down in a giant messy pile. Or organize them in neat piles and name them after your dogs; I don't care, as long as you can't see them. Going clockwise, take turns drawing a card and doing the following:

Ace: Choose any player to drink one.
King: Men drink one.
Queen: Ladies drink one.
Jack: All players drink one.
10: Second person to your right drinks one.
9: Second person to your left drinks one.
8: All players drink one.

7: Any player to the right drinks one.
6: Any player to the left drinks one.
5: Change the direction of play and everybody drinks one (social).
4–2: Drink the face value.

Accessorizing:

- Whenever two of a card have been drawn (keep the drawn cards on the side), double all drinks for the two remaining ones.
- Any player who draws the same card as the player before (e.g., Player One draws a nine, then Player Two draws a nine as well) gets to make up a rule. The rules can be anything from not saying certain words to doing something embarrassing, like uncurling your eyelashes or jamming a carrot in your vagina. Both are pretty standard.
- When a female draws a queen, her drink totals are tripled for three rounds.
- When a male draws a king, his drink totals are quadrupled (× 4) for three rounds.
- Every time an ace is drawn by a male, go around the circle naming action movies until someone can't name one; that person drinks four. (See Movie Requirements below for what makes an action movie.)
- Every time an ace is drawn by a female, go around the circle naming chick flicks until somebody can't name one; that person drinks three. (See Movie Requirements below for what makes a chick flick.)

Movie Requirements for Action Movies:

- Diabolical plan involving terrorists who want to take over a factory producing an element we've never heard of but that can apparently destroy "an area the size of Texas."

- Diabolical plan involving terrorists who are upset because their jawline isn't as chiseled as our hero's.
- Diabolical plan involving terrorists who take entirely too much interest in our hero and die in brutal ways after they kidnap his daughter, who ends up killing various bad guys in a coming-of-age kind of way.
- Diabolical plan involving terrorists to export cocaine out of Colombia as if no other drug exists in the world and no country but Colombia knows what drugs are.
- Diabolical plan involving terrorists who are angry about their phone bill because 1-800-DIABOLICAL-HENCHMEN-ARE-US started charging long-distance fees.

Movie Requirements for Chick Flicks:

- It is called *Pretty Woman.*

SHIT CREEK

Morning After: *"Last night's party must have been crazy! We have three MDAs (Mysterious Drinking Accidents), four UPIs (Unidentified Party Injuries), and I think Mark just spotted a few BBs (Beer Bruises). I'm surprised we didn't have any UHVs (Unconscious Hospital Visits) or RNPs (Random Naked People)."*

Players: You're gonna need more than one person to paddle, especially if one of you is drunk and reenacting the "Jack, I'm flying" scene from *Titanic* for the three hundredth time.

Supplies:

- A deck of cards
- Having a nose is good, but not relevant for this game

Beer: Enough to fill a creek, also known as that crack in your table that you float your bottle caps down

Objective: To make it across the creek without getting covered in shit

Getting in the "Water": Lay sixteen cards face down in a four-by-four square. Take turns trying to get from one side to the next without getting a jack, queen, king, or ace. Start from any side you want and turn over one card in each line as you make your way across the creek. If you turn over a face card in the first line, drink two. If you turn one over in the second row, drink four. Hit a face card in the third row and consume six; nail one in the fourth and final row and serve yourself eight. If you make it all the way across without getting a face card (a.k.a. stepping in shit) you get to hand out ten drinks to whomever you please.

Every time someone hits a face card, remove it and place another card face down in its place for the next person's turn. Also, you have to cross *in order* from the row you start in to the row farthest away, meaning you can't just draw the four cards in any order you like; you have to go in order as if trying to cross a river . . . of poo.

Courtesy Flushing:

- If you get too good at using just four cards (it's all luck, jackass) try using a five-by-five or six-by-six square.
- Try making each face card do something different than just making you drink. For example, have jacks mean that you lose an article of clothing, queens make all girls drink five, kings make all guys drink five, and an ace means the drawer can make up a rule.
- If at all possible, get someone so drunk he craps himself. Drink five for the irony.

Paddles: If you find yourself up shit's creek (feeling like shit) on a party night with no paddles (energy) but want to go up stream (party, tough style), use some of this clever and surprisingly helpful drinking jargon I've garnered over the years:

Take a Booze Snooze: A nap in the early evening to prep you for the night.

See a Drink Shrink: Someone who drinks so often he is wise in the ways of the booze and can help you with your PABS (Pussy Ass Bitch Syndrome).

Hair of the Owner: A close cousin of Hair of the Dog, Hair of the Owner is where you return to wherever it was you bought the drinks from last night (bar, store, etc.), thus returning you to the party-hardy state of mind you were in last night.

Preintoxication Masturbation: Not so much a clever name as a rhyming jump start to your evening.

Call the Ugly Train: This term usually applies to a mysterious train that takes away all the ugly people from the bar after you finish your eighth beer. In this case, it applies to the removal of all ugly feelings as you begin the night with a glass full or rum (yes, a glass).

Now go see the Grog Monster!

SUNSET

The Flamingo Code: Some people get drunk and fight, some get drunk and cry, and some wake in Newark with a stamped passport. Flamingos, however, paint. They get completely shit-faced and just paint. This is why they stand on one leg—they have to hold up that paint-holding tray thingy. At least that's how it was until Leonardo da Vinci stole a flamingo's painting of a beautiful girl named Mona and passed it off as his own. He then destroyed all their paint-holding thingies to cover up the truth: that Leonardo da Vinci was, indeed, a flamingo.

Players: Mammals and Fowls. Fuck reptiles.

Supplies: A deck of cards

Beer: The beer of flamingos: Heineken. Don't act like you didn't know that.

Objective: To guess correctly and not get jacked by the flamingo's beak

Setting Up the Canvas: Sit around a table, making sure the flamingo has room to ruffle its wings. The flamingo starts as dealer. Player One is the first dude on its left. The flamingo holds the deck in his wing upside down so no one, including itself, can see the next card. Player One then has four options:

Red: He can predict the next card will be red; if he is wrong, he drinks one; if he is right, he gets to hand out one drink to anybody, even the flamingo.

Black: He can predict the next card will be black; if he is wrong, he drinks two; if he's right, he hands out two.

Early Sunset: The flamingo turns over two cards, of which one must be red and one must be black; if he is wrong, he drinks four; if he is right, he hands out four.

Sunset: The dealer turns over four cards, of which two must be red and two must be black; if he is wrong, he drinks eight; if he is right, he hands out ten. This is to encourage more sunsets.

Interesting Facts: Flamingos don't migrate once each year—they migrate *daily*. Migrating is like coked-out sex to these birds. They are also responsible for creating sunsets. This is because flamingos, as they fly, shit themselves, spreading beautiful pink and orange droppings into the clouds. I'd also like to point out that nothing I just wrote has any factual basis.

Farewell: Well, that's all for this game, my friends and flamingos. And next time you look at a sunset, look closely and you just might see a beautiful flamingo, majestically spreading its wings, squatting, and crapping it out.

TRAPPED

Party Barge: Everyone knows the story of Noah's Arc, but not everyone knows how he pulled it off. I stumbled upon the truth after successfully getting a dog, two crabs, and a cat *completely shit-housed.* Noah was the inventor of wine (seriously) and knew, as I do, how to get animals drunk. Back in the day, there were no animal rights groups, so he could fuck up whatever creatures he wanted! So, right before the first round of global warming hit, he held an animals-only wine-tasting aboard his ship, the *Alcoholic Rum Connoisseur,* or the "Arc."

Players: Two of each kind of person. Interpret that however you like.

Supplies:
- Cards
- Ridiculing experience

Beer: Enough to hold you over until the locksmith gets there

Kinda Fun: Try to "trap" your hammered buddy in a small space and hold the door shut for a minute or two when he gets in. Drink one for every minute it takes him to realize it only locks from the inside. Then play this game to be ironic.

Objective: To be rid all of your cards first and not get trapped *too* often

Locking the Door: Deal out the entire deck evenly, everyone hiding his hand from other players. The person with the longest toenails starts the game. He can lay down any card he wants face up in the middle of the table. The next player must lay down a card of the same value or he is "trapped." When trapped, you take one drink for every card laid down until you are untrapped.

When you are trapped, the game revolves around you, just like a party would if you were blacked out and locked yourself in a bathtub (yes, it's possible). So, you become trapped, and you drink one. The next player then lays down a card that must be different from the first card played, and then it is back to the trapped player. He must first drink one because a card was laid down, and then he has a chance to become untrapped by laying down the same card as *that* player. If he *can* play the same card, he does so, drinks one for the card he laid down, and the game proceeds around the table until the next person gets trapped. If he *can't* match the second card laid down, he has to drink one more and the game keeps going around the table until somebody plays a card that the trapped player can match.

By the way, it can be ten to fifteen turns before someone gets trapped, so don't think you're doing something wrong if no one's drinking. This is what alcoholism is for—you should always be drinking.

Dead-Bolting:

- Each time someone gets trapped after the first, the drinks are doubled (the trapped player now drinks two for each card laid down while trapped). Games end when all cards have been played. Start back over at one drink per card in the second game. Or not.

- Each round before the game starts, you have to trade five cards with another player; this is where some strategy comes into play. You can try to get all four of one card so that you can automatically trap someone, or try to get one of each card so you never get trapped yourself.
- If you like, you can make certain cards worth more drinks than others. For example, if someone gets trapped with an ace, make him drink two or three for each card laid down, until he's untrapped.

A Quick Word on Alcoholism: Just because one of your parents is an alcoholic doesn't mean you have to be. All it means is that your parent has an addictive personality. This means you can be addicted to whatever you want! Cocaine, gambling, stealing—the sky's the limit!

WAR

The Hundred-Beers' War: *"'Twas a fortnight to be remembered. Actually, we were all pretty shitty, but you know what I mean. They fired their best Beer Pong cannons at our men, who are only alive today thanks to their powerful shields of Flip Cup and Chumbawumba skills. They held a siege, starving us down to our last twelve-pack, until our reinforcements arrived . . . drunken seniors from the bars! Armed with the growing fear of entering the real world, they pelted our enemies with comments like, 'How old are you, twelve?' With their spirits broken, we changed the song, stole their girls, and won the war."*

Players: Enough to fill the ranks. (Two, three, or four works best, depending on the size of your tank.)

Supplies:
- Cards
- Nuclear capability

Beer: A score

Objective: To get all the other players' cards. Also, don't get shot.

Charge! Deal out ammunition evenly to all soldiers. Nobody can look at his weapons. If there are more than four soldiers, I'd suggest using two firearms storages. There are no turns in war; each round, everybody fires the top missile of his armory into the battlefield. The general with the most powerful warhead wins and takes as his own all the other missiles launched.

Translation for the Pacifist: Everyone lays down the top card of his deck, face up, and the highest card wins, taking the others into a side stack for the next round.

Card ranking goes from the most powerful (ace) down to the least powerful (two). If two of the same highest card are laid down, its wartime, bitches!

War: Each player in the war (and there can be more than two) lays three cards face down and then one face up. The final card laid face up is the warring card that determines the winner. The winner of the war gets all the cards from that round: the two tying cards at the beginning, the six face-down cards, and the two final face-up cards. If the last two face-up cards are the same *again,* it's double war! If this happens, you both lay three more cards face down and flip another final card face up. This last card then determines the winner. If the card is the same *again,* which it most likely never will be, keep doing the same thing (three down, one up) until someone wins.

If you run out of cards to play during the war, shuffle the stack of cards you've won and start from the top of the deck. If you have no other cards, just lay down what you have and make the last card be the face-up determining card.

The game is fast moving and simple. The highest card wins the round; if there's a tie, you have a war. Every time you get through your initial deck, shuffle the cards you've won and start again. Not everyone will finish his stack at the same time because people will win different amounts. Pause to let the players shuffle whenever they run out, and keep going.

Here Is When You Drink:

- Drink one every time you lose a round. (Only one person wins each round, and rounds usually last about five seconds; you get drunk *real* quick).
- Drink two every time you lose a round and the card you played was the same suit as the winning card (if you played an eight of diamonds and the winner was a king of diamonds).
- Drink five for every lost war. Drink ten for every lost double-war and fifteen for every triple.
- Everybody drinks two if there is ever a jack and an eight played in the same round. Don't ask, just do it.
- Twos beat aces. Yes, that's right. Aces are not infallible and twos are not useless. If your ace gets beat by a two, you drink three. If there is ever an ace and a two in the same round, the two is always the most powerful, beating out any other cards played, as well as the ace.
- If you ever reach to grab the cards because you think you won but didn't look closely enough, drink one. Punk.
- Each time you shuffle your deck, drink one.
- If you ever actually finish a complete game and are still conscious, I applaud you and will finish my drink.

- If a girl's boob ever pops out, drink three.

Warning: If you do indeed play this game until someone officially wins *and* drink every drink required of you, you may find yourself waking up clutching mops and frying pans with a video of yourselves reenacting the Civil War in your kitchen.

WASTED EIGHTS

After playing this game alone for three hours straight one night, I embarked on an adventure of unimaginable imaginability. I was drunk, so naturally I started digging with the shovel I always carry when alone and hammered in odd places. I had only dug a few feet when I made a history-changing discovery: an ancient race of skeleton people. No skin, no organs—just bones. How did they drink? How could they hide their beers when the cops rolled in? I decided to forget about it and to just do what I normally do, and pee on them.

Players: Players ≤ 52

Supplies:
- Cards
- Being able to see helps

Beer: Eight

Objective: To be lucky

Let the Absurdity Begin: Deal everyone one card. However far away his card is from eight, each player drinks. So if you get dealt a three, you are five away (four, five, six, seven, and then eight) and therefore must drink five. If you get an ace, you drink seven (ace, king, queen, jack, ten, nine, eight). If you get either a seven or nine, you get to hand out three drinks. If you get an eight, you get to hand out five drinks. And yes, this is the simplest game of all time. People from *Vermont* even get how to play this game.

If you are feeling ballsy and don't like your card, you can choose to go double-or-nothing and get another card. You then have to guess what your next card will be. If you guess the exact value of the card or are within one, you're off the hook. You don't get to hand out any drinks, but you are saved from what you would have had to drink. If you don't guess close enough, you have to drink double what you would have in the first place. So if you had an ace, doubled down, and missed it, you drink fourteen.

Drinking Tactics: Try playing it to where you go around the circle clockwise, each round having a new person pick what card is the desired card. For example, Cock-Blockins could say three was the card you wanted, so if you got a three, you handed out five drinks; and if you got a two or four, you'd hand out three drinks. It's also ballsier because, if you pick three as the desired card, you can drink a lot more if you get a king or ace.

Royalties on My Discovery: This is the official statement by me, Alex Bash, saying that my discovery of the recently peed-on skeleton people will not be a vanity find, but one for the betterment of humanity. Go forth, my friends, and find out all you can about this amazing race before it's too late and we, too, God forbid, become skeleton people. Although I have to say, I wouldn't mind seeing the phalanges on Scarlett Johansson! Right, guys!?

DiCE GAMES!!!

1–2-3

Isn't it odd how the number one has the lowest value of any number, but everybody wants to be #1? How everyone wants to finish first, instead of, say, 3,968th? The answer, like all mysteries, stems from beer. See, One was an alcoholic; like, big-time alcoholic. Like, keg-a-day keeps the memories and liver transplant-list away alcoholic. The day all the Numbers met to decide their values, One was drunk and spent the day naming his toes. It was on this fateful day that Roman Numerals ambushed the Numbers' meeting and knocked them out stone cold. One, having given up on remembering his ten toes' names, stumbled around town and passed out in the chalked-off square reserved for the highest value. By the time the other numbers came to, it was too late. This is why, when people win, they often get drunk.

Players: Three, four, five, or more

Supplies: One, two, three, or four dice

Beer: One, two, three, or more twelve-packs

Objective: To roll a six at the opportune moment

As Easy as 1–2-3 Drink! I can't think of an easier game. This is for all those dicks who would roll the dice a certain way to get a six during board games. Like that little prick Jack . . . I swear, if I ever see him again, I'll saw off his balls and . . . anyway! The game moves clockwise very quickly, with each player rolling one die on his turn, one roll per turn; and no matter what he rolls, he passes it on. However . . .

The first player to roll a six chooses how many drinks the person who rolls the second six must drink. Keep in mind that the person who ends up drinking could just as easily be the one who chose the number of drinks. The game moves really fast around the table, with someone occasionally rolling a six, calling out a number, then everyone else shouting like a banshee when someone rolls the second six.

6 . . . 6 . . . 6:

What the third six means is up to you. Choose what the final Mark of the Beast means from one of the following options:

- Whoever rolls the third six makes a rule that all players have to follow or else they drink a chosen amount. The fourth six starts back over as the first.
- Every time the third six is rolled, choose a letter from the alphabet—any word starting with this letter cannot be spoken. A one-drink penalty applies for each use.
- Choose a basic word like *the* or *that* or *uvula*—every time this word is spoken by the third six-roller, everybody has to salute him until the next third six is rolled. Last one to salute His Royal Uvulaness drinks one.
- Third six-roller: kindly remove an article of clothing.
- Give the third six-roller the power to make someone do something truth or dare style.
- The person who rolls the third six cannot touch his head (including the face) for the remainder of the game, with a two-

drink penalty per touch. Sound odd? Try it. You'll be no less than browned out* in half an hour.

1 IN 300

There is a 1 in 300 chance that some douche-bag asteroid will hit Earth on December 24, 2029, at 9:47 P.M. This is a Friday, so be sure to be partying up your last night, doing that mundane activity called "being alive." For every person you see flipping out and screaming, "The world is ending!" drink two. You'll be sure to be *smashed* before being *smashed* . . . literally!

Players: Works best with four or more.

Supplies:

- Six dice. But three or four could work, too.
- A daring, adventurous spirit

Beer: Well, the title does say 300 . . .

Objective: To be able to come up with a bet that is so complex and rambling that no one realizes the odds are approximately 465 to 1

---

* Brown out: As opposed to "black out," when you remember nothing of the previous night's events due to overconsumption of alcohol, when browning out, you may recall vague instances but no details.

Example: "Last thing I totally remember, I was doin' jager-bombs with this chick from Chi Omega and we went upstairs but I think I threw up or jumped off the arboretum bridge with Ralph and the guys—anyway, it was awesome. I think I may have set someone on fire . . ."

Through the Atmosphere: I'm gonna be honest, there's no reason why this game is called 1 in 300, except for that it has to do with odds. But, I guess, so do most dice games.

On his turn, each player chooses how many dice he wants to roll (one to six). He bets a certain number of drinks that he will roll a certain something. He doesn't have to include *all* the dice and he doesn't have to be too specific. He can bet however many drinks he wants for whatever roll he feels like. It's up to the other players to either take the bet or say, "No way man" (read: "You're a fucking idiot").

For example, Player One could say, "I bet four drinks that at least two of my six dice will land on *six.*" If Player Two disagrees and thinks the odds are too poor for this to happen, he can call his bet. If Player One does indeed roll the two sixes, then Player Two drinks four. If Player One rolls one or no sixes, then *he* has to drink four. Since Player One said, "*At least* two of my dice will be sixes," it's okay if he rolls three or four. It's up to the player whose turn it is to decide if he wants to specify a certain number.

Anybody who is decent at math will be able to at least somewhat figure out what bets are good ones to take and which aren't. Or, if you're feeling daring, bet a high number of drinks and make an outrageous claim; it's the most fun part!

If the player whose turn it is can't get anybody to take his bet because it's too crazy, he can either pass the dice on, which makes him a gigantic wad of gayness, or alter his bet and predicted roll to make someone call him. Or, he can just take his own bet and either drink the drinks himself because he lost, or hand out the drinks he won to himself.

Betting the Housed:

- Make sure your bets are unique and not boring ones like, "I bet two drinks I'll roll at least one three with these three dice." That's boring. Try something like, "The closest die to Bob will be either three or four, and the closest die to the edge of the table will be higher than two." These are also more confusing and make it tough for the other players to calculate odds.

- If two or three players call the roller's bet and the roller loses, he doesn't have to drink double or triple his bet. However, if he bets four people and wins, each person who called his bet has to drink four, not split them up. This encourages people to make crazier bets and not be so reserved.

Dealing with Morons: If any of your friends actually thinks the asteroid, which has a 1 in 300 chance of wiping out mankind in 2029, is going to hit the Earth, get him drunk and in his bed, turn off the lights and start shaking the bed like an earthquake. He'll wake up, still drunk and disoriented and scared as hell. Hold a mattress up against his bed so he can't get out the side, trapped in a sort of cushy pod. Yell that he's been in an alcohol-induced coma for twenty-one years and that an asteroid is about to hit earth. Hold red paper in front of the light and flash it like an alarm is going off. If you do this, e-mail and tell me about it, and I'll drink ten.

Clichéd city to be shown destroyed by asteroid: Paris

Clichéd structure to show after world has ended: Statue of Liberty

Clichéd reason we couldn't stop the asteroid: Incompetent government

Clichéd effect on people killed by asteroid for no reason whatsoever: Turn into zombies.

7 ATE 9

"I prayed to my beer last night—is that bad?" I'm asked this question more often than, "How are you?" Granted, it may be because I'm the "drinking games guy," but it also could be because the answer digs deeper than the meaning of life itself. See, ever since Jesus turned water into wine, he and alcohol have been connected much like Harry Potter and Voldemort. This is why, when you drink heavily, you feel like you're in heaven, and when you wake up in the morning with no alcohol inside, you feel like hell.

Players: Two or more

Supplies:
- To have taken, but not necessarily passed, algebra
- Two dice
- A really tall glass

Beer: Seven or nine should do. Fuck eight beers.

Objective: To roll a seven. Or anything else.

Swallowing: Players take turns rolling both dice at the same time. If a player's combined roll equals seven, they get to pour as much beer as they want into the "really tall glass" mentioned in the **supplies** section above. This is also called the "community glass" or the "fuck me up, Scottie" glass.

If a player's dice total equals eight, he has to drink half of the beer in the community glass, and if his roll equals nine, he has to drink it all. There is a five-minute limit for all drinking, each player only gets one roll per turn, and the turn moves on no matter what that player rolled. If the roller rolls anything but a seven, eight, or nine, nothing happens.

The only other mandatory rule is that when someone rolls doubles (including two fours), the order of turns is reversed and now goes counterclockwise.

If you get too bored with my simple rules (jerk) simply make up different rules to go along with each number. For example:

- If someone's roll equals three, he has to run around the room singing "Mary Had a Little Lamb" in a Jamaican accent.
- Snake eyes means finish your drink, obviously.
- Double-sixes? Choose someone to finish his drink and then roll again, Mr. Badass Roller.
- If a roll totals five? Sing and act out "I'm a Little Tea Pot" in the front yard.
- When someone rolls two fives, he tags someone and both players race out of the room to find a deck of cards to build the best card tower they can before all other players finish their drinks. Highest tower wins.
- You get it. Be creative. And if you're not creative, you obviously haven't drunk enough yet.

The Beer's Prayer:

Our Beer, which art in boxes
Budweiser be thy name
Thy twelve-pack come, thy keg be done
At home, as it is at college
Give us this day our daily drunk
And forgive us our vomit
As we forgive those who have vomited on us
And lead us not into hangovers
But deliver us Bloody Marys
For thine is the party, and the sing-along,
and the memories, for ever and ever.

21 ACES

Time Travel: Like most highly scientific and abstract concepts in life, the question of time travel can be solved by studying alcohol. Drinking is a system depressant; when we drink, the body slows down. When we continue to drink beyond what is safe or reasonable, the body slows down so much that it passes beyond complete stasis and into the realm of hyperspeed, where it joins the speed of light at 670,616,629 miles an hour. Sadly, science has yet to figure out why our bed or couch can stop this travel, or why we so frequently misplace our cell phone during the process.

Players: You and a couple of buddies

Supplies:

- Money and beer. Toss in ESPN and call it a life.
- A die

Beer: Actually, hard alcohol may work better.

Location: A bar or a home with a stocked liquor cabinet

Objective: To roll the sixth, twelfth, twenty-first "ace"

Changing the Future: It helps to be of legal drinking age or have a good fake ID. Just don't go to Pioneer Square. So, you and a couple of your buddies are sitting at the bar or at a table and have a die. Take turns rolling it, between making derogatory comments about ex-girlfriends and the stock market. Keep track of the number of 1s that have been rolled. One roll per turn; pass it on no matter what.

The person to roll the sixth "1" (or "ace") gets to pick the shot that someone is going to drink. This can be anything from a shot of Jager to a double 252 to a Four Horsemen. The person who rolls the twelfth "ace" get the honor of paying for the chosen shot, and the person to roll the twenty-first ace gets to drink it.

If you aren't of legal drinking age or got your fake ID taken by that dick who didn't believe you were of Moroccan descent, don't fear, you can still play at home. There's a few ways to go about the "paying for the shot" part. You could have everybody buy his own fifth or pint, and if you roll the twelfth ace you have to offer up a shot of yours. Or, you could all pitch in for a fifth of something really nice and whoever rolls the most twenty-first aces gets to drink more than his fair share.

Digesting the 8:

- Make sure you keep track of the aces so no one claims that he rolled only the eleventh or thirteenth ace, or that he rolled the twenty-first ace and tries to take the shot. To keep track, try using bar peanuts, pretzels, beer caps, bras, or animal sacrifices. Or pencil and paper, I guess.
- If you're not doing anything but playing the game, it can get kind of boring, so play to where whoever rolls an odd-numbered ace has to also drink five.

Avoiding 7 and 9:

#1 tip about fake IDs for guys: Backward hats, backward hats, backward hats. Every eighteen- to twenty-year-old guy looks the same in a backward hat.

#1 tip about fake IDs for girls: Have big tits.

BEER DIE

Press Release: New York, NY—At 3:15 A.M., Beer Die was walking down the street when he saw a cowardly bottle of flavored vodka dressed in black grab a purse from an elderly woman. Beer Die sprang into action. He chased the vodka down a back alley, over a rusty fence, through an army boot camp practice base laced with barbed wire and land mines, before finally tackling the fleeing bottle and taking the purse back to the elderly woman. Unfortunately, by the time he got back to her, she had passed away. Beer Die, being the emotional guy he is, used her money to buy himself beer and drink away her memory.

Players: Four players, two teams of two. No more, no less. Unless you wanna play with more, which is fine.

Supplies:

- Four keg cups
- One six-sided die
- A flat rectangular table
- Four armless chairs or two benches (preferably)
- Hand-eye coordination
- Mouth-cup coordination
- Throat-stomach coordination
- Sober-drunk coordination

Beer: You do not need enough beer to make you die, but an alcohol-induced coma isn't out of the question.

Objective: To be the first team to get seven points or make the other team tap out

Not So Basic Basics: Teams sit on opposite ends of the table facing each other; players have their respective keg cup in front of

them. Fill each keg cup with one beer and set it on the table in front of you. You determine where the cup goes by placing your elbow at your corner and letting your forearm lay on the table while clenching a fist. Your cup goes on the inside of your fist, usually about a foot and a half down the table and a few inches in. Roll the die to see who goes first.

The first team up picks a player to go first, doesn't matter who, and they try to throw the die underhand into one of their opponent's keg cups. The die must go as high as the table is long to count as a legitimate throw. If the die does not go high enough, the opposite team can call "height" and stab the die-tosser in the thigh for his insolence. Metaphorically, of course. They must however call "height" before the die hits the table, for it to count.

If you throw the die and it lands in one of the opposite team's cups, both of its players have five minutes to drink their beers down. When you make it into a cup, it is called a "plunk," and this is the one exception to the "height" rule. With plunks, it does not matter how the die got into the cup: whether it was too low, off the ceiling, or bounced in, it still counts as a plunk. Plunks are very valuable 'cause they get the other team drunk, so they can't throw or catch the die as well. It also makes you be able to convince them the score is 5–2 in your favor as opposed to 6–1 in theirs. Tell them they could be the Comeback Kings. This will excite their primitive minds.

When the die bounces in, call it a "pussy-plunk" because they didn't earn it. Make sure to make them feel bad, as if they'd cheated.

This brings us to points. Points are scored when the die is thrown high enough, hits the table, and then bounces off the far edge and is not caught. If the die bounces off the side, it is ruled a "side-out." This is sometimes argued about when the die goes off near the corner, so try to watch carefully and don't lie and say it was a side-out if it wasn't. If the die is not thrown high enough and is not caught, it is not a point. It helps to have good, fast hands in Beer Die because dice can bounce in crazy ways, especially when the table resembles a fucking bombing field from years of dice and pongs being cast about.

If you throw the die and it hits either of the opposite team's cups but does not go in, it is called a "plink," and counts as one drink, which that team's players must consume immediately. There are six drinks per cup. If the die hits the cup and then goes off the edge and is not caught, it is *not* a point. If the die bounces off both cups, it counts as two plinks.

If you throw the die and it misses the table completely, either off to the side or too long, your team must drink one. There is no penalty for a throw where the die lands on the table showing anything other than a four (explained below).

The game is over when a team gets seven points, and you must win by two. There are many, many more rules, technicalities, and strategies, which are listed below.

Try Not to Die:

- In case you didn't notice, both players on a team always drink together.
- If at *any* time the die lands on the table and a four is facing up, your team must finish their cups. This may be after you threw

it, hit it, or simply placed it down to go piss. "Fours," as they're called, are unlucky because sometimes you plink their cup, which is good, and then it rolls back onto a four, which is bad because you have to drink your whole cup while they only drink one. Commence pondering of karma.

- When catching the die, you *must only use one hand*. If someone uses two, give him a warning the first time; after that, it counts as a point. If the die happens to land somewhere like your leg or crotch or something, you must roll it off into your hand as you stand up or roll over or whatever you need to do to make the die roll off you. You can't just pick it up as you can a hooker.
- When I say you can't use two hands, that only means to catch it. You can bobble and juggle the die all you like. Some of the most amazing catches are when someone hits it and sends it flying and has to dive off the bench to catch it. Expect to see this on ESPN's Top 10 in the coming years.
- When you are plunked, keep the die in the cup as you drink it because, when you finish, you have to roll it out of your cup onto the table. If it's a four, drink up—again. If not, carry on with your turn.
- You can never touch the die before it goes off the table either on your edge or as a side-out. This is interference, and whichever team interfered drinks one and gives the die back.
- If you only have three drinks left in your cup when you are plunked, you just finish your three drinks. You don't drink any from the next round.
- Make sure to keep track of the score as best you can, as games can last an hour or two and people will get drunk and forget. I suggest putting a beer up on a pedestal for each point you score, so there's no way anyone could forget. Also, beer deserves to be on a pedestal, so you are doing it in honor.

- Before the game starts, make up a rule for if someone accidentally plunks themselves. This can be as simple as just drinking his cup, or as crazy as making him go streaking around the block. Oh and, Duncan—you need to trim, bro. Seriously.
- You can never trap the die against your body or anything else. For example, you can't slap and hold the die against your chest. However, in my experience, catching the die in your cleavage is often waived.

Now for a Little Strategy . . .

- The whole point is to win by getting to seven points first. However, what really turns out to be the goal is to get the most plunks and plinks. As you're throwing, try to look right down your arm and line it up perfectly with the opposing player's cup. If you have no arms, I hope the money from the lawsuit settlement was worth it.
- Hold the die with three fingers: your thumb on the back and your middle and index finger on the front. Release it as if a flower is blooming. Bees and pollen are optional.
- If you have a tendency to throw slightly to one side, try going for the opposing player's cup that is diagonal from you.
- Make sure that you and your teammate have an understanding of who's going to catch the die, depending on where it goes. Pick sides, and if the die hits that side for whatever reason, that side's person catches it. No matter what. It's of course okay to help each other if one person bobbles it, but I have a little friend named Mr. Tea Bag waiting for you if you infringe on my territory without merit.
- If you just want to get points, try to put some mean spin on the die when you throw it; this causes it to bounce all crazily and makes it hard to catch. Losers will accuse you of "being cheap." Fuck them.

- Once you get good, have a game of trick beer die, where you only throw the die from behind your back or between your legs or with your other hand. Or, set two tables super far apart and try bombing the die overhand like a grenade.

Literal Beer Die: If you ever manage to play beer die with ten-person teams, using barrels of beer and basketballs for dice, call me. I'll be on the next flight.

DICE

Should-Be Felons: All the hoopla around drunk driving has taken away the gusto from a less deadly but much more frequent felony: drunk walking. Even though the U.S. drunk walking limit is a BAC of 0.3 percent, many surpass this and continue to walk on the right side of the sidewalk. This leads to, among other things: knocked over shopping carts,* slightly delayed partygoers, frightened squirrels, and death. When a friend gets too drunk to walk I urge you all to take action and, much like taking away a driver's keys, sever his legs.

Players: Enough players to form a synchronized swimming team. If you know how many this is, put down my book. Seriously.

---

* I have personally been involved in a serious drunk-walking accident. I was being pushed around the Greek system in a shopping cart like normal, when someone who was Walking Under the Influence strayed into my lane, knocking me into a wall and giving me an awesomely huge scar on my shoulder, which, since then, has apparently come from saving children, helping old people, knife fights against terrorists, and a really, really sharp nipple.

Supplies:
- Two dice
- A cup

Beer: One to six

Objective: To drink and be merry

Basics: Take turns clockwise around the table, rolling both dice at once. First rule is, each time you roll the dice, you have to yell, "Diiiiiiieeeeeccccaaaaa!!" (pronounced Die-eee-sah). It's hilarious when people who are usually shy or reserved yell stupidly at the top of their lungs. If someone forgets or chooses not to, he drinks five.

This is a game where stuff happens depending on what the dice add up to. If your two dice are . . .

1–1: Take a shot of your favorite poison (vodka, rum, whiskey, ejaculation).
2–1: Nothing. Pass the dice on, sucker.
2–2: Doubles! Drink four, bitch (2+2=4).
3–1: Nothing. Pass the dice on.
3–2: Nothing. Pass the dice on to a more *qualified* player.
4–1: Nada. *¡Pase los dados!*
5–1: Your roll equals six; drink two.
4–2: Your roll equals six; drink two.
3–3: Your roll equals six; drink two. Also, you rolled double threes, so drink six as well (3+3=6).
6–1: Your roll had a six in it; drink two.
5–2: *Nothing!!!* Please kindly hand off the dice. Fucker.
4–3: What a boring roll. You have no soul; pass them on.
6–2: Your roll had a six in it; drink two.
5–3: Wow. Pass them on and stop talking.
4–4: Hooray! Drink eight (4+4=8).
6–3: Your roll has a six in it; drink two.

5–4: Nothing . . . ? Yup. Pass 'em.
6–4: It's got a six, drink two.
5–5: Two fives! Drink 10! (5! + 5! = 10!)
6–5: Drink two. You know why.
6–6: Get to ready to have a Cheez Whiz fight. Drink four for the two sixes, drink twelve for the dice equaling twelve, and drink a shot of your choice for the double sixes.

See? Pretty simple. You drink two whenever your roll equals six or has a six in it. You take a shot for 1–1 and 6–6, and you drink however many your doubles add up to. That's it. Have fun. Give me a call later. I'm writing a book of transcribed drunk dials and would appreciate a few after playing this game.

FIVES

The Results Are In: Nine is the sexiest number. Although three and eight were in contention with their vague likeness to boobs and seven was in the running for its common usage in money and gambling, nine takes the cake. Why? It's powerful (ever seen a price tag without two nines?), it can be a six *or* a nine (great for the sexually experimental), and lastly: nine is the atomic number of fluorine, a highly dangerous chemical, and let's face it—danger is sexy.

Players: Five works best.

Supplies:
- Five dice
- Kindergarten-level math skills

Beer: 5 × 5 should do.

Objective: To roll fives or numbers that add up to five and to remove your dice as quickly as possible.

Get Rollin': Players take turns rolling all five dice at once. When the dice land, remove any dice that are sitting on five or that add up to five (if you have a three and a two, remove them both). Use the numbers to get as many dice off the table as possible. Roll the remaining dice and repeat the removal process. Keep rolling whatever dice remain until you have none left (this may mean rolling one die over and over until you get a five). Your turn keeps going until you get all the dice removed.

The important thing is to keep track of how many times each player has to roll the dice. Say it takes Player One fifteen rolls to get them all gone. It's now Player Two's turn. He does the same thing Player One did, while everyone keeps track of how many rolls it takes him. If Player Two takes eighteen rolls to get rid of them, he drinks three because he took three more rolls than Player One. If he takes only six rolls to get rid of them, then Player One drinks nine because it took him nine more rolls.

Summary: If the next player gets less than the first, the first player drinks the difference. If the second guy gets more, he has to drink the difference.

When Player Three rolls, his number of drinks is determined by the number of rolls it took Player Two to get rid of them all, and he drinks accordingly. Player Four's drinks are based on Player Three's and, if there is no fifth player, then Player One's next turn is based on Player Four's number of rolls. Basically, everyone's turn is based on the one before his, so try to sit to the left of the dumbest person. If everybody wants to shake your left hand, it's probably you.

This Isn't Nam, There Are Rules!

- You may not use the same die for two different totals of five. For example, if you roll two sixes, two ones, and a four, you can't use the four for the first 4–1 combo *and* the second 4–1 combo. You'd only remove the first four and one and then roll the remaining three dice.

- Yes, 6 + 4 = 10; no, you do not remove the two dice as if they are both fives.
- You can play this game with any desired number in place of the five. I suggest thirty, but that's just me.
- If you want the game to move faster, you can play with rules like, "If you roll two fives in the same roll, you get to remove a third die. Or, if you roll three of the same number (such as three sixes or three fours), you get to remove one." Decide this based on all players' combined desire to get smashed.

Quick Survey: Does anyone else wish the so-called nerdy card game Magic: The Gathering was more socially acceptable? No? Fine; screw you, guys. I didn't want to go out anyway. I've got orcs and dragons and elves and tears and loneliness to keep me company!

FOLVF

One day, the drinking games Golf and Fives got drunk and spent all night long under the sheets having loud, raging, hot, sweaty, passionate discussions about life. They also had sex and gave birth to Folvf, a clever combination of both their names, which neither of them could properly pronounce, so they named him Bill and put him up for adoption, like any fourteen-year-old parents would do.

Players: At least four

Supplies:

- Five dice
- Paper, to be used as a scorecard, and a pencil, so you can erase your score when everyone else is too drunk to notice

Beer: Two or three should be sufficient to get a solid buzz. Oh, and that's two or three *twenty-four-packs.*

Objective: To roll a bang-load of threes

Going Folvfing: Before you start, decide whether you're going to play nine holes or eighteen. Write down the hole numbers on the left-hand side of the scorecard and make a column for each player next to each hole. On each player's turn, he rolls all five dice. Remove any threes or dice that add up to three (a one and two would both be removed). After you remove the allowed die, add up the face value of the rest. This is your score. As in golf, you want the lowest score possible. You only get one roll per turn, so make it count. After you roll the dice and add up your score, write it down next to "Hole 1" and pass them on to the next player.

After each hole, the player with the lowest score is the winner, and the rest have to drink the difference between their score and the winner's. So, if the winner got a score of five and you got thirteen, you'd drink eight.

You may not use the same die for multiple add-ups. For example, if you rolled two fours, two ones, and a two, you could not remove both the first 1–2 combo and the second 2–1 combo. You'd just remove one of the ones and the two, and then roll the remaining three dice. Also, a six does not count as two threes.

Keep playing each hole as you did the first one. The drinks and scores for the second and third holes have nothing to do with the first one. You could lose the first hole by ten "strokes" and win the second hole by just as many. After the ninth or eighteenth hole, add up all the scores. This is where big-ass drink sessions can take place. The winner is crowned Ultimate Folvf Champion of the World, while the rest drink the *entire* difference between their final score and the winner's. So, after eighteen holes, if the winner's total is 126 (averaging seven strokes per hole) and your total is 180 (averaging ten per hole) you'd drink 54. Trust me, it can be much, much higher than this. I think the most I've seen is just under 100.

Then, it's time for round #2! Hooray!

Gameplay Suggestion: I don't feel like working out the odds but, if you are so inclined, you could figure out what the average "strokes" per hole is. I guess you'd do this by finding the average number of dice that get removed in the first roll, and then finding the average total of the second roll. Then, you could play independently of each other and drink one for each stroke over par, and hand out one drink for each stroke under.

Weekend Afternoon Suggestion: Mini-golf + nalgenes of mixed drink = crazy good times

LOW MAN

Why Dice Have Six Sides: In 2100 BC, fifteen brave alcoholics battled the evil prohibitionists in the Burnt City. Their balance was off but they felt no pain as they blindly swung at whatever wasn't blurry or spinning. Although they were outnumbered 500 to 1 and covered in their own bodily fluids, God loves drinkers so he decided to smite the soulless prohibitionists. However, from either the gaping impalements or alcohol poisoning, six alcoholics died. In their memory, God created the six-sided die and invented Low Man so we could drink away the pain.

Players: Very minimum should be five.

Supplies:

- Two six-sided dice per person. I know it's a lot. Cry about it.
- A mouth gag (to silence prohibitionists)

Beer: Ten different kinds works best, but ten of the same works, too; you'll see why.

Objective: To not roll the lowest total

Clearing Your Memory: Line up the ten drinks in a row, labeling them #2 through #11. There is no #1 because two dice cannot add up to one, and there is no #12 because, if you roll two sixes, you get a super-special prize! The drinks do not have to be in any order, nor do they all have to be beer. Actually, it's better if they're not.

Everybody rolls two dice at the same time while yelling, "Boobies!" together. Nothing brings you closer together than yelling, "Boobies." The person with the lowest total says, "Fuck!" and rolls both dice again. The total of this second roll determines which drink he will drink from. If it totals five, he drinks from the #5 drink; if it totals ten, he drinks from the #10 bottle, and so on. Whatever drink he has to consume from, he takes down five. If there is a tie for lowest combined roll, both players drink.

The only exception is if the initial lowest-roller rolls a twelve (double sixes) on his second roll. In this case, he gets to pick someone to roll again and drink double (ten) from the serendipitously numbered beverage.

If the chosen player rolls double sixes yet again, it shoots back to the original loser, who has to roll again and drink triple the amount (fifteen). If he miraculously rolls twelve again, you should probably do some sort of ritual to get the demons away. Also, the dice are given back to the guy who rolled twelve the second time and he has to drink quadruple the usual amount (twenty).

Carrying Out Their Dreams: It is best to play this game in a loud room where everybody's drunk and yelling and dice are bouncing everywhere and people are going, "Ooohhh!" when somebody rolls double sixes. It's also fun to play at a socially unacceptable dinner party where nobody is yelling and the only thing bouncing are your friend's bail checks as they try to get you out of jail for being a "public disturbance."

25-CENT MATHEMATICIAN

Quarters Are the Shit: They start your laundry, feed your parking meter, and hurt more than other coins when dropped from elevated locations. They also make girls bend over to pick them up, and if you're desperate you can even buy a paraplegic Taiwanese hooker! Just kidding! But not really!

Players: Two. Any more is just silly.

Supplies:
- A quarter
- Two dice

Beer: Amount = cosine multiplied by the tangent

Objective: To make your die and quarter equal more than your opponent's

Basic Addition: Before you start the game, decide who's going to be heads and who's going to be tails. Roll to see who gets the quarter for the first round. Each round, both players roll their respective die at the same time, and somebody rolls the quarter along with their die onto the table. Whoever has the lower number showing on their die drinks the difference (if Player One rolls a three and Player Two rolls a six, Player One drinks three).

However, whichever side the quarter is showing, the player with that side gets +1 to his die's number. If Player One rolls a four and Player Two rolls a two, but the quarter reads "heads" and that was Player One's chosen side, he now has five, and Player Two drinks three instead of just two.

Oh, and if you tie, you both drink the number you tied at.

Each "round" should last about a minute, with the majority of the time going to drinking your owed drinks. It's a really fast game my friend and I made up when we were trying to get drunk really fast before going to a movie.

Beyond the Dice:

- A roll of one beats a roll of six. It's like David versus Goliath, and makes ones not completely worthless. In this case, the quarter does not matter. If a one and a six are ever rolled together, the one wins straight up, the quarter is obsolete, and the six-roller drinks five.

- If you want to get drunk even faster, try using an eight-, ten-, or even twelve-sided dice. Again, make sure that a one beats the highest possible roll.

- Play with two or three quarters if you want to make it more interesting. Or, use two dice each.

- Say, "Weanus!" every time you roll the dice. Or not.

MEXICO

Ahhh . . . the stereotypically wonderful Spring Break location of college students everywhere. Get legally wasted in public and pass out on some beach after winning a wet T-shirt contest and taking a four-hour booze-cruise with best friends you just met. You also get the chance to experience waking up halfway to Liberia in a black market organ trafficking ring . . . that you're in charge of! *¡Si si! ¡Muy bien! ¡Bolígrafo! ¡Saca Punta! ¡Pollo!*

Players: Four to six players works splendidly.

Supplies:

- A nontransparent cup
- Two dice

Beer: *Mucho Cerveza*

Objective: To roll better than the player before you or convince him that you did

!Tiempo de Partido! The guy with the most girly name or the girl with the most manly name goes first. Player One puts the two dice in the cup (which no one had better be able to see through!), shakes it around, and slams it down on the table, concealing the dice beneath it. He then peeks under the cup without letting anyone else see and says what the dice read. If everyone else believes him, he is good to go and passes on the cup and dice to the next player, still not revealing what he rolled. If someone thinks he's lying about his roll, they can call him out on his bluff. If they wrongly call him out, the accuser(s) drink three; if they correctly call his bluff, the liar drinks three.

How a roll is read: the higher number of the two dice is the "tens" number, while the lower is the "ones" number. A roll of

5–3 is read as 53. The number 35 does not exist, and no, you cannot choose to read it this way. A roll of 3–4 is 43, a roll of 5–6 is 65, and so on. The highest roll possible that beats all others is 1–1, even beating out the second-highest roll, 6–6.

The object is to roll a higher roll than the person before you. Say Player One rolled a thirty-two, or so he says he did, and we all believe him because thirty-two isn't really all that great. Player Two must now roll (or say he did) higher than thirty-two or else he has to drink three. Say he rolls a twenty-two, but only he knows this; he can say, "Yup, beat it with a forty-three." The other players can choose to believe him, in which case he passes the cup and dice on and no harm done, or they can call his bluff and make him drink three. If they call his bluff out and they are correct, the next person's roll has to be higher than Player Two's *real* roll of twenty-two, which he revealed when they called his bluff. If you tie the previous roll, you lose, so if you say, "Tied him with a thirty-two," you are both stupid and will be getting hammered.

Currency Exchange:

- It may be a strategy to say, "Beat him with a sixteen . . . whoops, I mean sixty-one, or, wait . . ." because this will make the other players think you're bluffing and call you out.
- Be ballsy. The reason it's only three drinks if you incorrectly call a bluff is so that people do it more often.

Mexican Hangovers: A major obstacle of partying hard in Mexico is the hangovers. Granted, they only last for about thirty minutes until you start drinking again, but they are vicious nonetheless. The reason is twofold: you can't drink the water because it's dirty as fuck, and the damn sun wakes you up at six A.M. every morning because Mexico doesn't believe in shades.

Advice: Drink heavily moments before passing out so you're actually still drunk when you wake up (and not just, "Dude, I think

I'm still drunk," after a regular party night). Cuddle with tequila. Wake up and give it a capless kiss.

Honestly . . . I have no idea why the game's called Mexico.

MY CALL

Offensive Science: Many things happen when a female gets pregnant. Her stomach expands, she becomes irrational and moody, she gets cravings for random kinds of food . . . oh, wait—that's when she's drunk. Or is it both? I was two years into a study on the differences between drunken and pregnant girls but had to stop abruptly when I mixed up my notes because both sets looked *exactly the same*. This is why doctors urge pregnant women not to drink: the world would implode with insanity.

Players: Three plus

Supplies:
- A cup
- A die
- A quarter

Beer: It's your call.

Objective: To call the right side of the quarter and come up with new variations to make the game more interesting

The first Trimester (three drinks deep): Take turns shaking up the quarter and die in the cup. The player to the shaker's left calls out whether he thinks the quarter will be heads or tails. The player shaking the cup then rolls the die and quarter onto the table. If the next player called the quarter correctly, the player who rolled it drinks however many the die is showing. If the guy to the roller's left called it wrong, he drinks however many the die is showing.

The Second Trimester (6 drinks deep): Try using two quarters and having the guesser call them both.

- If he guesses both correctly, the roller drinks double what the die is showing.
- If he guesses only one correctly, then both roller and guesser drink the die's value.
- If he guesses them both wrong, he drinks double the die's value. Your call, right?

Racing to the Hospital (Racing to the Hospital): Craps! Try playing My Call like the gambling game Craps, where everyone plays off the dice roller. Get a bunch of drunken rowdy people standing around wagering drinks on what the quarters and dice will land on, roll, and then watch as everyone tries to remember what the hell they just wagered.

Random Fact of My Call: If you are an average American, in your whole life, you will spend an average of six months waiting at red lights, unless you're a taxi driver, in which case you will spend six minutes, and only because you rear-ended an Oldsmobile and your engine exploded.

RISKY BUSINESS

Sneaking in Alcohol: There will come many a time in an Imbiber's life that he will need to sneak alcohol into somewhere: sporting events, dinner parties, dances, movies, church, and so on. Although there are many decent tactics (down the pant leg, pocket inside purse, butt of boxer briefs) there is only one truly fail-safe way to get alcohol through the door: become the town's alcoholic, so nobody questions it. Get started by playing this game.

Players: 4.67. When you get drunk you'll understand.

Supplies:
- Six cups
- One die
- A mouth

Beer: As much as your failing heart desires

Objective: To become one step closer to getting public assistance for being a real, diagnosed alcoholic

Sneaking In: Line up the six cups in the middle of the table and number them one through six. Take turns going clockwise, rolling the die once per turn. Whatever number the die shows is what cup you're going to be dealing with. If the cup is empty, fill it up with as much beer as you like. If it's got some beer in it, drink it down. Be careful filling the empty cups, because it could be you pounding them.

One more rule: When you're drinking the cup down, there's no stopping. It's got to be all in one chug. That was my roommate's idea. Blame him.

Getting Out: The advanced version of this game (Business So Utterly Stupid It Comes with a Chance of Death) has the same six cups but uses four dice. Everyone takes turns the same way but instead rolls all four dice . . . :

- The die closest to the roller's body determines the cup.
- The die second closest to the roller's body is how many drinks he has to drink.
- The next-farthest-away die (third) is the "gambling die." If the roller thinks he can beat what the die is showing (i.e., get higher by rolling it again), he says so and rolls away. If he beats it, his drink charges are dropped; if he doesn't beat it, then the drinks given to him by the second die are doubled.
- Double whatever number the fourth and farthest-away die is showing. If it's an odd number, the roller drinks that many; if it's even he gets to hand out that many.
- If three of the four dice are showing the same number, the roller adds them together and hands out that many drinks.

Risky Business' favorite haikus!

Quick drinking lesson:
Do not try to eat your phone
Stomach does not ring

I know I'm not drunk
Because there is not fat chick
In my car's backseat

Drinking lots of beer
Hitting on my neighbor's wife
Oh wait that's my dog

How to change a bulb
Place the bulb into its hole
Drink until room spins

COIN GAMES!!!

ANCHORMAN

A Tragedy Explained: Most think anchors were created to keep ships in place; this is a lie. It's what drink-happy captains told the public to justify having a gigantic cool-shaped keg on board at all times, and Edward John Smith (ill-fated captain of the *Titanic*) was about as big an imbiber as they come. As the *Titanic* approached the iceberg, people tried to use the anchor to slow it down, only to discover the truth: they were going to be the most happily drunken people to ever drown in the icy waters of the Atlantic Ocean.

Sailors: Two teams of four, with nine total (you'll need "that guy" there to yell random shit).

Supplies:
- Eight quarters (try not to dip into savings)
- A large pitcher of beer
- Soap. Gotta keep those hands clean, right?

Beer: Another large pitcher of beer

Objective: For your team to bounce all your quarters into the pitcher first

Setting Sail: Ahoy, fuckers! Divide into two teams of four, each sailor with his own quarter; if he loses it, he has to "walk the plank" (get hit in the balls by a humorous object). Set the pitcher of beer in the middle of the table and position each team on opposite sides.

Both teams count down together from three in a very dramatic Hollywood-like fashion. When they get down to zero, both teams try like deranged livestock to bounce their quarters off the table and into the pitcher of beer. First team to get all four quarters into the pitcher wins; the other team has to pound the pitcher. Here's the catch: the losing team must pass the pitcher from the first player to the fourth player (a.k.a. the Anchorman), but each player can only bring the pitcher to his lips once, and the Anchorman has to finish whatever is left in the pitcher.

Repeat.

Hoisting Your Sails:

- Make sure the Anchorman is either your best drinker or the most naive freshmen with no tolerance, so you have someone's back to play tic-tac-toe on when you run out of paper.
- I said "soap" in the supplies section because, although I personally don't really care, some people don't like the thought of eight dirty quarters sitting at the bottom of their drink.
- You can play this game with teams of any size, but make sure to correctly scale the size of the pitcher so everybody gets thoroughly intoxicated.
- If you're too good, try using two or three quarters per person so the rounds last longer.

Drinking Tip of the Anchorman: That stupid drunk test where you place one foot in front of the other is nothing compared to actually walking across something as skinny as your feet, like a tree branch, a passed-out guy's arm, or a stolen road sign used as a bridge to get from one side of the Communication Building's roof to the other.

AUTOMATIC ASSAULT QUARTERS

"'Twas a dark, quiet night at Pi Kappa Alpha, unless you count the three hundred or so partygoers rampaging through the halls, creating drunken memories they'd never tell their spouse, except The Hamster: he wanted revenge. After an unprovoked water-balloon incident at an intramural Ultimate Frisbee match, he craved to get his assailant, TwoHole, very drunk very fast. He knew what had to be done. He narrowed his eyes, positioned his hand, and sank his quarter into the large glass. Handing it off to TwoHole for the fifth time in a row, he knew, in not too long, he'd be drunk enough to draw a full-scale penis on his forehead."

Players: Four to ten

Supplies:
- One small cup for each player
- One quarter for each player
- One large cup
- EQBS (Extreme Quarter Bouncing Skills)

Beer: The better you are, the less you'll need.

Objective: To bounce your quarters into whatever cup you can

Safeties Off! Give everybody his own quarter. The first player to eat his quarter wins a six-pack and an enormous hospital bill. Then . . .

Sit everyone around a table. It doesn't matter where you sit because there are no teams. Set the large cup in the middle of everyone, and set one small cup in front of each player. Everyone pours a little bit of his own beer into the large cup, filling it to the brim. Then, everybody fills the smaller cup in front of him with his own beer, and let the games begin! But first get your hands out of your pants!! Use some vodka to cleanse them! Of course it works!

Okay, you count down together and then, at the same time, everyone tries to bounce his quarter into either the small cup in front of him or the large cup in the middle. There are no turns, so all the players just start rapid-firing their Automatic Assault Quarters. If you make it into your small cup, you get to hand it to whomever you want. He needs to drink it down (faster, bitch!), give you back your quarter, and refill the small cup up with *his* beer. This is why the better you are, the less beer you'll need, because you'll be using everybody else's!

If you make it into the large cup (which should be very, very difficult), you get to hand it to two guys who get the pleasure of downing it together. This is how friends are made; through pitcher-chugging, not friendly meet-and-greets.

Man Down! If you are getting the quarters in too frequently (Joey's trying to flush the refrigerator handle within twenty minutes), get some bigger cups. The fridge should only flush after an hour or two of playing.

"Only the dead have seen the end of war . . ." Chill, Plato. If you need to have a winner at the end of the game, make it so each time someone gets his quarter into the large cup, he earns a point; first one to five or ten or fifteen wins. "Only the drunk will see the end of this war . . ."

If Beer Replaced Guns: There would still be wars, but they would be significantly shorter and probably cost less money (but only if Doritos are on sale). There'd be endless lines of men and women vying for a spot on the front lines. Discarded bottle caps fill the trenches. Tanks fire giant Ping-Pong balls into garbage cans of beer. Stealth bombers drop millions of dice into millions of keg cups; waves of Budweiser wash over our troops. Homeless Harry signs up to fight for his country. Alan the Alcoholic is made general. Ireland is a force to reckon with. Love, exaggerated boasts, and slurred, never-to-be-fulfilled promises fill the air.

BIRD OR MAN

Police Report from the Nest: *"A crow was arrested this morning after blowing a 0.32 percent on the beakalyzer test. At 4:35 A.M. on the upper west branch of the Forty-fifth Street oak tree, Officer Squawk got reports of a boisterous crow claiming he was a bald eagle and had crapped on every car in the Wal-Mart parking lot. Officer Squawk confronted the crow, who in a span of fifteen seconds confessed his undying love for hummingbirds, broke into tears, and pissed his feathers. Determined cause of intoxication: the drinking game Bird or Man.*

Players: Condors, phoenixes, blue jays, and cardinals only. No robins. . . . Pricks.

Supplies:
- Feathers, nest
- One quarter

Beer: No beer, just worms. . . . Covered in beer.

Objective: To correctly guess what side the quarter lands on

Leaving the Nest: The person with the lamest last name (general consensus) starts the game by spinning the quarter on the table, taking a drink, and then smashing it down underneath his palm before it stops spinning. He has to spin the quarter, take a *full* drink, place his beer back on the table, and not be touching it before he can slam the quarter. If the quarter stops spinning or goes off the table, he has to drink two and spin again.

When he eventually gets it slammed down under his palm so no one can see it, he peeks at the quarter, and then points at someone to guess whether it's a bird (tails) or a man (heads). The quarter spinner also must yell, "Bird or Man!" in the most horribly obnoxious voice possible. These get funnier and funnier as the game goes on. If his voice is not obnoxious enough (general consensus), he drinks one and tries again.

If the player he pointed to is correct, the spinner has to drink three and pass the quarter on to the guesser. If the guesser is wrong, then he has to drink three, and the spinner has the option of keeping the quarter or passing it on to the guesser. It can be a good or bad thing to be the spinner, depending on how you look at it. On one hand, you have the ability to make others drink if they guess wrong. On the other hand, you have a spider. Smush it. You also have the possibility of drinking amounts of alcohol the surgeon general would most likely not recommend.

Worst Five People to Meet While Drunk:

5. Ex-girlfriend (unless she's a slut)
4. Boss (unless she's a slut)
3. Government official (unless she's a slut)
2. Esteemed Political Figure (unless she's a slut)
1. Police Officer (unless she's a slut)

DRUNKEN MORON

In terms of awesomeness, being perpetually drunk is somewhere between complete euphoria and a four-hour orgasm. In terms of coordination, it puts you somewhere between a mentally impaired ape and a toaster. In terms of carrying coins between your butt cheeks, it places you somewhere between your-friends-will-never-let-you-forget-how-fucking-stupid-you-looked and your-friends-will-never-let-you-forget-how-fucking-stupid-you-looked.

Players: As many as you can; this game is hilarious.

Supplies:
- One quarter
- A small cup
- Knees
- Butt cheeks (as needed)

Beer: Be sure to have already drunk some before you begin

Objective: To drop the quarter from between your knees (or butt cheeks) into the cup below, which apparently has a forcefield

Learning to Wobble: Set up a small runway about ten feet long, depending on how drunk and uncoordinated you are. Just make sure there is a distinct starting line and then place the small cup on the ground at the finish line.

Players take turns holding the quarter between their drunken knees and trying to drunkenly walk down the entire runway without dropping it, the ultimate goal being to get it into the small cup at the end. If you complete this goal, you choose three other people, playing or not, to chug the rest of their drinks, because you are my hero and I am in love with you.

What will more likely happen is you'll drop the quarter somewhere along the way. You then walk from the quarter to the cup by placing one foot directly in front of the other and counting how many steps it takes. This number is how many you drink.

If using your knees proves too easy or you just want to show off how talented your ass is, trying squeezing the quarter between your butt cheeks and waddle down the course. Whether you wear pants when you do this is on you.

Greatest Suggestion Ever: All I can say is: have races.

FREE THROW

People, we need to start taking better care of our water, which, as we all know, is a vital ingredient in beer. If we keep tarnishing our water, how will breweries keep making beer? I've got goose bumps just thinking of it. And then, think about this—if there's only enough water to make beer, how will we drink some before bed to dull our hangover? What about wet T-shirt contests—milk?! What about summer afternoon drunken slip 'n' slide adventures?! How are we gonna peg cars with water balloons on the viaduct?! I urge you, for the sake of our drunken sanity and see-through white T-shirts, please, save the water.

That is all. Now let's go booze as much as we can before it runs out.

Players: Several

Supplies:
- One large glass
- Six or seven shot glasses
- A thumb and index finger

Beer: If you're not trying to do some crazy shit this evening, use only beer. If you feel like sneaking into Husky Stadium and shotgunning on the fifty-yard line, grab a little hard-A as well.

Objective: To bounce the quarter into the large mug

Going to the Line: Sit around a table, place the large mug full of beer in the middle, and completely surround it with shot glasses either half-full of hard alcohol or all-the-way full with beer. Each person has two bounces per turn to try to make the quarter into the large center mug by bouncing it off the table and in. If you make it into the large center mug (which should be very hard to do), choose someone to drink it down. If you miss and it lands or bounces into one of the shot glasses around the mug, *you* get to drink it. If you fill the glasses all the way up with liquor, you will die, so don't. If you miss everything all together, shoot again with no penalty. You get two bounces per turn whether or not you get the quarter wet.

If you need to have someone "win" because you're insecure about yourself, make it so the first person to land in the mug ten times wins. Keep track on paper because you *know* you'll get drunk and forget.

Suggestions My Friends Made Me Put In:

- If you're really good or just really want to get hammed, make two "layers" of shot glasses around the center mug as if a bulls'-eye, creating an even higher chance of landing in one.
- As you can see, using liquor in the shot glasses will get you faded way faster than using beer. May I suggest having some full of beer and some half-full with vodka?
- There would be a third suggestion here from my friends/researchers but it was entirely too stupid and I would most likely be sued.

Suggestions I Put In:

- Try psyching each other out as fans do when a basketball player is shooting free throws but, this time, don't hold back your keg cup full of beer. What's the worst that could happen? If they throw a cupful back at you, you'll get to take off your shirt and show off the abs you've earned by being too perpetually hungover to eat anything!
- Bouncy balls

LAND MINES

Here's What I Think: Instead of filling real land mines used in war with explosives, we should fill them with cases of beer. This way, when the enemy steps on them, cases of Budweiser fly out. I can see them getting drunk and realizing how stupid war is, making peace and puking on one another. They would then be forced to surrender under the premise, "Dude, fighting back after we gave you beer would be *such* a party foul."

Players: The more the better. Seriously, like, fifteen plus is *great.*

Supplies:

- A flat table (the smaller it is, the drunker you'll get)
- Two quarters

Beer: The larger the cans, the better; you'll see.

Objective: To successfully spin the quarters, drink, and pick them up before they stop

Semi-Automatic Shot-Gunning: You want to start the game as sober as possible so you can drink as much beer as fast as you can during the game. Everyone sits around the table, taking turns spinning the quarters. On each player's turn, as the quarters are spinning, he has to take a solid one- to three-second drink, put his beer down on the table, and pick up both quarters before they stop or fall off the table. If he messes up on the spin, can't pick them up in time, or grabs them before his beer is down on the table, he has to do it again, drinking every time.

Here's where the land mines come in. When a quarter is spinning, anyone can slam it down onto the table with an empty beer. So, when it's not your turn, you should be drinking heavily so when your roommate's quarter is spinning and he's drinking, you can reach over and slam down your empty beer on the quarter, thus making him go again. The empty cans slammed down *cannot be moved* for the duration of the game. They are now land mines and will hopefully fuck up people's spins. The more land mines that get put on the table, the higher the chance someone's spinning quarter will hit one and burst into a fiery explosion of several more drinks.

It's up to the rest of the players to determine whether someone's beer was down before he snagged the quarters (hint: it never was). It's okay to still have your hand on it, but it has to be on the table and you actually have to drink and swallow while it's spinning, not just hold the beer up to your lips.

Bomb Plans:

- If you're shooting and chasing, feel free to slam down the empty chasers as well. Two-liter bottles work well. Having ten two-liter bottles with only a few ounces left in each works even better. If you finish a keg, you should probably call an ambulance to have your stomach pumped, but before you pass out and vomit your pancreas into your girlfriend's lap, slam it down mightily, my friend—you've earned it!
- Gang up on someone and build a fortress of land mines around him so he has to spin the quarter and drink fifteen or more times for every turn. But we're way too mature for that, right?

Perfect Prank Setup: Work with the person sitting next to you to drink as many cans as possible and hide them beneath the table. Then, when someone is already half-past hammered, slam them all down during what will be his last turn. Watch him spin twenty-plus times without getting them up. As always, I expect pictures.

War Reparations: If you get a midget blacked out and cover him in tinfoil and use him as the quarter, end your life. You will never experience a greater moment.

NICKELS

Three pieces of advice for things that sound fun while drunk but end up sucking:

1. Fire extinguishers are meant to *set off* fire alarms as well as put out fires, so no, do not frostify Charlie for spilling your beer.
2. Trying everybody else's drink to "just try it out" is fine until you get mono and glandular infection, lose twenty pounds, and can't "try" much of anything for two months.
3. Streaking down a main avenue + bike cops = hilarious for those watching, bad for you. Wear your clothes *to* the desired location, then strip. Amateurs.

Players: Three to five

Supplies:
- Two nickels
- A flat surface (not your hair, moron)

Beer: A kind you can drink quickly

Objective: To spin the nickels correctly and slam one down

5 Pennies None the Richer: The player with the hottest girlfriend goes first. If no one has one, you can't play. Kidding; choose somebody. The first player takes all two nickels, puts them together as if trying to make them look like one, and spins them as he would a quarter. If you don't know how to spin a quarter, you probably shouldn't play this game. If someone doesn't know that this game involves spinning coins, force him to play. He is up first.

The spinner can either screw himself over or get someone else exceptionally drunk. He spins both nickels at once. They both must spin at the same time long enough for him to yell, "I have illegitimate children!" and then slam one down before they stop spinning. It doesn't matter which one he slams down, but the other one has to still be at least moving, even if it's almost stopped. If he fails to do any part of this (a nickel doesn't spin properly, one flies off the edge, he can't slam one down fast enough, etc.), he drinks two. If spinning two is too hard, then just use one. And then hand over your testicles; you don't deserve them.

After slamming one down, he points to his victim and says, "Guess." The chosen player must then guess if the nickel is showing heads or tails. If he's wrong, he drinks two and the current spinner keeps going; but if he's right, he gets the nickels and does what the first player did.

As in curling, there are no winners. Just a bunch of drunk idiots pushing round objects. Ouch! Just kidding; curling is rad. My friends and I used to watch curling and drink three every time a rock knocked another out of contention.

New Rule: Drink three every time a nickel knocks another nickel out of contention.

SPEED QUARTERS

2008 Track "Quarter" Finals: They ran hard all year, these two quarters, and it was down to the final race . . . before the semifinals and finals, of course. Fifty cents would start the race, twenty-five would finish a champion. The stadium was filled with disappointed fans who didn't know it was literally the *quarter* finals. The winner would go on to fame and fortune, masquerading around with half-dollars and shiny young nickels; the loser would get stuck in a gumball machine. It was then they realized they were inanimate objects and started some dude's laundry.

Players: Between eight and four. Who says the lower number has to go in front?

Supplies:

- Two keg cups, or two glasses of the same size that are relatively easy to bounce a quarter into
- Two quarters

Beer: Enough to cover your soon-to-be-passed-out body

Objective: To make others drink. Is there a better objective?

3 . . . 2 . . . 1 . . . GO! Two people sitting across from each other start with an empty cup and a quarter per person. They rapidly try to bounce their respective quarter off the table and into their respective cup. The point is to get the quarter into the cup as fast as possible. When you make it in, you quickly pass it to the person on your left, who immediately starts bouncing away. If the other cup catches up to you, you must "stack" the cups by placing one behind the other and bounce the quarter into the farthest cup on your first try, or you drink five. It's in your best interest to get the quarter in and pass it on as soon as possible, so the other cup doesn't catch you. This is why it's called *speed* quarters.

Here's the best part: If you make the quarter in on the first try, you can slide it to anyone you want (who doesn't already have a cup). This means that if you and the guy across from you start with the cups and you make it in on the first try, you can pass it to the person to his right, thus potentially screwing your opponent. Or, you can slide the cup to the person on the first guy's *left,* thus screwing this new guy, because odds are that the first guy who started with the quarter will make it in before the guy who just got the cup does.

Strategy:

- Gang up on somebody. I know it's not exactly great for brotherhood or friendship or mental stability, but it's hilarious to have one guy scrambling to get the quarter into the cup while everybody else is making it in on the first try and passing to the guy right behind him.

- If ten or more people are playing, then invite me over—this sounds like fun. Also, I'd suggest using three cups. And yes, with three cups you can be triple stacked.

- If you have terrible outbreaks of obsessive-compulsive disorder and you must take everything you read literally, then get a flat surface, tilt it, and let the quarters speed down its slanted surface.

Tips for the Newly Alcoholic Athlete: You are not faster when you sprint while drunk; that's the car you're riding on top of. You are not a better basketball player while drunk; that was an empty swimming pool and you dunked a gallon of Rossi. You are not a better fighter; that was a fire hydrant, and you lost. You are not a better baseball player; just because no one can hit your pitches doesn't mean you threw a perfect game. You *are,* however, a better drinking games player, so turn the page and win that trophy! (Trophy not included.)

SPINNERS

Genesis III: And there was the Earth, rotating around the Sun just like God made it, but the whole "gravity" thing wasn't working out too well. One day, God was spinning a heavenly quarter on his heavenly table, and a heavenly mosquito landed on it, but didn't fly off due to the heavenly gravitational force of the spinning quarter. Thus, He pointed His heavenly finger at the Earth and said, "Spin, bitch." And the Earth, being God's bitch, began to spin just as it does today.

Players: Anywhere between 2 + 2 and 5 – 1

Supplies:
- A table small enough that everyone playing can reach any part of it
- A quarter

Beer: Enough to make you spin. (Ha! Clever? Maybe?)

Objective: To spin the quarter and not be a douche bag

Quarter 'til Drunk: Whoever's parents hated him the most when they named him starts the game, and yes, that means you, Billworth. Billworth starts with the quarter and spins it on the table while everyone makes fun of him for his name. Before the coin even slightly begins to stop spinning, Billworth must call out the name of someone playing. The named player must quickly stop the quarter with his index finger while it's still on its edge, as if freezing it while spinning. If you don't get what that means, then ask someone, because it's hard to explain. Imagine how James Bond would stop a quarter; he wouldn't slam it down, he'd smoothly touch the spinning quarter ever so lightly so it stopped under his index finger. Then he'd have sex with it.

If the spinner makes the quarter go off the table, fucks up on the initial spin, or fails to call out a name before the quarter begins to slow, he drinks two. This is called the "Don't be a douche bag" rule and must be strongly enforced. The point of the game is not to wait until the quarter starts to fade and then call out a name.

If the named player messes up while trying to stop the coin on edge, he drinks two and the quarter remains with the original spinner. If the named player correctly stops the quarter, he has to spin it from the stopped position. Maybe this paints a visual of how the quarter must be stopped; you can spin the quarter again from the position in which it stops.

Besides that, have fun, don't be a D-bag, and try to end up with at least three pictures you wouldn't want the cops to see by the end of the night.

Quarter Past Drunk: If you ever get "the spins" from drinking too much, spinning the opposite way *will* indeed counteract it. Go ahead—try it! I'll be over here, starting a betting pool as to how soon you will puke.

SUPER QUARTERS

"Oh No, My Cat!" An underdressed, large-breasted woman's cat was stuck up in a tree. "Fucking cats," thought Super Quarter. He used his large, muscular ridges to climb the tree as the damsel below looked upon with admiration. Heroically braving the blistering wind and rain, he moved his metallic body within inches of the terrified cat. The cat, seeing a giant metal monstrosity coming at it, jumped and fell to its death. Super Quarter shrugged and popped a cold one.

Players: Six plus

Supplies:
- One cup for each player, all the same, all relatively small
- One quarter for each player

Beer: Lots; keep it next to you, close to your heart. Literally.

Objective: To become the ultimate quarter-bouncing champion of a lifetime. Intrigued?

Magnificent Quarters: This is the fastest-moving game ever involving coins. Everybody stands around a table and starts by filling his cup with a drink or two of his beer, or about the maximum amount he can drink in one large gulp. Everyone counts down to zero and then starts frantically trying to bounce his quarter off the table and into his cup. If he makes it, he passes it right away to the player on his left, who must fish the quarter out, drink it down, fill it back up, and start bouncing again. *But,* he must first make his original cup and pass that on before starting on the cup just passed to him. It doesn't matter on what bounce you get your quarter in, just get it in and pass it as fast as possible.

The whole process of drinking, filling, and bouncing shouldn't take more than five or ten seconds. It is possible, if you suck, to get a line of cups waiting for you to drink and plunk, but it's unlikely because odds are, somebody else isn't making it in on the first try either. Even if every cup caught up to you before you made your first one, you'd only have to pound six or so drinks and you'd have all the time in the world to make the cups and pass them, because no one else will be bouncing.

It may sound a little confusing, but it's not: just hectic. Quarters and cups are flying this way and that and no one really keeps track of what's going on. You could have three cups behind you and not even notice, but it's fun, and should probably be accompanied by loud, fast music.

Stupendous Quarters: To best bounce a quarter, hold it between your thumb and index finger and bounce it down against the table, trying to make it land as flat as possible with maximum surface area hitting the table. Nobel Prize, here I come . . .

Lousy Quarters: To most improperly bounce a quarter, get really drunk, pass out, and get your hands tied behind your back, then wake up in a drunken stupor and attempt to play Super Quarters by holding the quarter between your teeth and slamming your head into the table.

RIM JOB

Definition: The term *rim job* has a somewhat disgusting meaning. It's when someone buys a large tube of lubricant, puts on dirty clothes, wets his lips, gets down on his knees, sticks out his tongue, and polishes the rims on his car's tires. Simply disgusting.

Players: Less than five

Supplies:
- A tall glass
- A dime and a quarter
- Finesse

Beer: Cheap beer for yourself, something nice for the middle

Objective: To bounce a coin into the glass without touching its rim

Rim-Jobbing: Everybody has his own side beer to drink from; fill the middle glass with something really nice and expensive that everybody pitched in to buy. Play a giant game of paper-rock-scissors to see who goes first.

Player One tries to bounce the quarter or dime off the table and into the glass *without it touching the rim of the glass*. This is the most important part of the game. Regardless of whether the coin goes into the cup or bounces off, if it hits the rim of the glass, the bouncer drinks three and passes the coin on to the next player. This game is all about the perfect bounce. If you can bounce the coin into the glass without it touching anything but the table and the sweet liquid inside, you get to drink the entire contents of the middle glass. So, the better you are at perfectly bouncing coins, the more you get to drink of the expensive drink you all pitched in to buy.

Regardless of what happens, each player only gets one bounce per turn. On each player's turn, he can choose to bounce either the quarter or dime. The quarter tends to bounce higher and more accurately, but the dime is smaller and has a lesser chance of hitting the rim of the glass. Life is full of hard decisions.

If you bounce the coin and it doesn't touch the rim but hits the inside of the glass before splashing into the liquid, you get to drink two from the glass and all the other players get to put "almost" in front of everything they say to you, as in, "I'm almost going to not pee on you tonight."

If your coin bounces off the outside of the glass or misses it completely, you drink one and pass on the coin. Keep in mind while choosing the large glass that it must be tall enough for it to be very hard to bounce a coin into perfectly but also must be doable, or you're all just going to pound one-drink rimmers until you pass out.

Questions, Class? Why does it have to be a glass and not a plastic cup? So you can hear the coin hit the rim or inside wall, jackass. Never doubt my infallibility again.

Cheat Sheet:

- *Tip #1:* Girls love the name of this game.
- *Tip #2:* Not really.

Rim Job: A form of oral sex involving contact between the anus of one person and the mouth of another.

TAPS

Drinking Buddies: I have a friend who I drink with every night, and we always said we'd be there for each other through the shots of Bacardi, the happy-hour chicken wings, and the overweight friends of attractive girls we wanted to meet. But last night, I looked at our beer-covered footsteps back from the bar, and there was only one pair (*tear*). So I asked him why, when I needed him most, there was only one pair of footprints? He replied: "Alex, when you see only one pair of footprints heading back from the bar, it was then that I carried your drunk ass; you're fucking welcome."

Players: At least four. This game is fun.

Supplies:

- A coin for each person
- The ability to be completely silent
- The shamelessness to tell Marty the Mute that he can't play because he has an advantage

Beer: Quiet beer . . . ?

Objective: To not mess up

¡Silencio! Sit in complete silence. If you so much as burp, fart, laugh, chortle, or hiccup, you drink one. Everybody should have one coin; it doesn't matter what. Anybody can start; turns move clockwise. On each player's turn, he has two choices: to tap his coin on the table once or twice. If he taps the coin once, the turns keep going clockwise (the player to his left goes next); if he taps it twice, the order gets reversed and goes counterclockwise (the player to his right goes next). Whoever's turn it is has approximately one second to tap his coin or he has messed up and has to drink.

The game goes around the table very, very quickly like a ticking clock on crack. All you hear is "tap, tap, tap-tap, tap, tap, tap, tap-tap," really fast until someone messes up, in which case he drinks three. If someone messes up, it is okay to speak up and say, "Drink!" However, if you incorrectly call someone out because you messed up and thought it was his turn but it wasn't, you have to drink three, as well as one more drink for speaking out of line.

Silenzio! Try playing a really funny movie in the background so people will be more likely to laugh and have to drink more, then get drunk and mess up and have to drink even more! Go easy on the volume.

Stillhet! (Sorry, I didn't mean to shout that.) Seeing as though farting counts as making noise, maybe a chili festival could be a pre-funk for this game . . .

Stille! Try playing with your eyes closed. Supposedly if you eliminate one of your senses, others get heightened. However, I don't think the scientists who figured that out used gin as a variable. When are they gonna learn?

MiSCELLANEOUS GAMES!!

20 QUESTIONS

How the "?" Was Formed: People never used to ask questions, which is why so many shitty governments stayed in power: there were no such thing as question marks! They did, however, yell a lot, so there was high demand for exclamation marks. One day, Mr. Exclamation Mark got so tired of being used that he drank his sorrows away. Later, he was bent over stumbling around town in the shape of a *?* and a peasant asked, "What the fuck is that?" This was the beginning of questions, revolutionary rebellions, and this very next game.

Players: One on one, teams, guerrilla militias vs. organized armies, or the like

Supplies:
- Your mind
- The human thought process

Beer: A modestly fair and averagely equal amount or so

Objective: To guess the item the other player is thinking about or to pick an item that the other player cannot guess

Basics: To see who goes first, put one or two fingers behind your back and make the other person guess. Whatever he guesses, cheat and win. Since you won, you get to pick an "item." This "item" has to be a noun. You cannot choose "up" as your item.

You also can't do something fucking stupid like "towers" instead of "tower" and make the person say the exact word. This is called "being a douche bag" and earns you three drinks for each question it took the guesser to realize you cheated.

The other person's goal is to guess your item by asking twenty yes or no questions. No question can be answered with anything except a simple yes or no. If you chose the item, make sure it is feasible to answer the questions; if you find that it's impossible to answer yes or no, or it's way too far of a stretch for the answer to be a simple yes or no, choose a different item.

When you are the guesser, you drink two drinks for every question you ask, so there's a minimum of two drinks (if you somehow guess it first try) and a maximum of forty (if you just barely get it). If you're obsessed and simply have to get it right, you can choose to go beyond twenty questions, but they are now five drinks a piece. If the guesser gets your item within the twenty-question limit, drink three for each question he had left before their twentieth. So if he got it on the seventeenth, drink nine, and so on.

Hard Items to Be Guessed: Metaphysics, modular commodity chains, tactical segmentation, hegemony, the Federal Fair Packaging and Labeling Act of 1987, monopolistic doctrine, the word *a,* post-Fordism new-era marketing, tax reformation, Transnational Corporation, time-space compression, vertical integration, and soup. Basically anything you had to Wikipedia the crap out of during college.

Some Excellent Questions:

- "Is your item a form of neoliberalism?"
- "Could I masturbate with your item?"
- "Could it be absorbed through osmosis?"
- "Would it be used after a subjunctive pronoun?"
- "Could I seduce my boss with it?"

- "Could it be used to hide your body in my trunk?"
- "Could you use the word *constructionalism* to describe it?"
- "Could it be considered a sex position?"
- "Would it feel good in my pants?"

Note: None of the suggested items or questions are legitimate.

BEER ROULETTE

National Geographic Documentary: "*Look at that beauty . . . the Samuel Adams in its natural habitat. Surrounded by beautiful women, doused in life-giving ice, and ready to be drunk by a real man . . . oh no, not the fashion designer, not the fashion designer! The Samuel Adams is about to meet a most painful death at the lips of a metrosexual! Here he is, seen popping the top, raising it to his lips and—*" (Text deleted due to X-rated graphics.)

Caution: Seriously, be careful; don't hurt yourself. Close your eyes when you open the beers and don't point them directly at your face. There's nothing worse than being drunk at a hospital on the island of Antigua with beer shrapnel in your cheek.

Players: Six, preferably

Supplies: A small box

Beer: Several six-packs

Objective: To not pick the shaken-up beer

Loading the Gun: Put six beers into a box and pull one out. Shake it up, and I mean *shake it.* Shake it so much you are scared to shake it anymore in fear of its blowing up in your face. Put this beer back into the box, close it, and *softly* shake the box just enough to move the beers out of place but not enough to shake up the others. Then:

Put on your favorite dramatic soundtrack.

Open the box.

Everybody grab one beer.

Put your beer to your head like a gun.

Open it.

Somebody is getting soaked; the other five are drinking a beer.

This is beer roulette.

BOAT RACES

Life Lesson: When you're on your deathbed, what will you wish you had more of in life: fun, right? This is why alcohol is the #1 invention of all time, because everything is more fun if alcohol is involved, including the other nine best inventions: drinking away the pain of infection (penicillin), boozing by the train tracks (steam engine), getting lost in flashy lights (electricity), chasing bubbles as you pee (plumbing), looking at Internet porn while drunk (computers), *The Simpsons* drinking game (TV), drunkenly throwing water balloons at cars (automobile), drunk dialing (telephone), and knowing that my drunken words can be spread to millions (printing press).

Players: Even-numbered teams

Supplies: One keg cup for each player

Beer: Seriously more than in any other game in this book

Objective: For your team to finish first and be thoroughly prepared to hate yourselves tomorrow

Hoisting Your Sails: This is the ultimate speed-chugging contest of a lifetime.

Line up the teams on opposite sides of a table. Fill each keg cup two-thirds full with beer. Choose which end is starting. The players at the starting end count down to zero, cheers their beers, and start to pound them. The object is to finish your beer as fast as possible.

To answer your question ahead of time: yes, you're going to be balls-deep in Ms. Drunk.

When you finish your cup, place it upside down on top of your head. This is to ensure everyone finished his entire beer, or else he gets drenched. The penalty for dumping beer on your head is getting beer dumped on your head. If your team is losing, you can sacrifice yourself and pour your full beer on your head to catch up or get ahead. Hell, you could all just dump your drinks on your head and win every time!

Like a relay race, the second person cannot start chugging before the first person has his cup upside down on his head. The first team to have all their empty cups atop their head wins and should probably pay a visit to the toilet or shower.

Speed Boat Variation: Instead of having one big-ass cup of beer per person, if you have enough shot glasses, fill ten with beer for each player, line them up, and have each player take 'em down one at a time, making sure to slam the first one down before he picks up the second one; trust me, way more dramatic.

Cruise Ship Variation: One word: straws. Oh yes.

Alex's Top 10 Inventions of All Time:

10. Battle-axes: killing people just became 66 percent more badass
9. Suffrage: giving women the right to be just as horny as men
8. High Bridges: giving suicidal people one last moment of fun
7. Viagra: fuck you, whiskey dick
6. Sharp Objects and Accidents: saving the gene pool
5. Football Season: the ultimate justification to daytime drinking
4. Lying: keeping me out of jail since age twelve
3. Jockstraps: saving my nuts since 1874
2. Nipples: no explanation necessary
1. Alcohol: enhancing every aspect of life by 8 billion percent

BODY PARTS

Inflation: Everybody is worried to death about the inflation of the U.S. dollar. What we really need to worry about is inflation in Monopoly money. Boardwalk and Park Place are losing property value, Baltic and Mediterranean have been repossessed, and the Luxury Tax has skyrocketed to 85 percent! Free Parking costs $10/hour! Community Chest is bankrupt! Somebody stop the madness!

Players: As many as you like; the more the merrier.

Supplies: Nada

Beer: Hopefully, a lot

Objective: To quickly name a body part nobody else has said yet

Stretching Out: Everybody sits or stands in a circle, lounges around a room, whatever—just know whose turn you go after. Whoever can name the most beer companies goes first because he is the man. This great person starts the game by saying a body part. You can name a muscle, a bone, a section of the body, random shit like an eyelash or fingernail, whatever you want.

Go around the circle clockwise with everybody saying a body part when his turn comes. If someone can't think of one, takes too long, or repeats one that somebody else said, he drinks five and the circle continues with the next person. Very simple, very fun, and very easily turned into other games like "sex positions" or "famous running backs" or "felonies committed by current players." That last one may take awhile.

Cooling Down: If thinking up body parts proves entirely too easy then you (a) aren't drunk enough, (b) are an anatomy major, and/or (c) should do one of the following to make it more difficult:

- Say each body part in a different accent.
- Wiggle a body part every time you name one, but not the one you named.
- Spell each body part; have Google handy.
- Start counting at one with the first body part and say the next number for each part thereafter, like, "Arm one," "Butt two," "Trachea three," "Fallopian tubes four," etc. It gets distracting, trust me.

Hanging with the Drunks:

- If you want to get smacked in the face by Mr. Drunkenness quicker, choose particular regions of the body to name from, like "lower body" or "reproductive organs" or "body parts most likely to be rendered unusable by a runaway go-cart."

- If you want to get smacked in the face by *Ms.* Drunkenness, tell her she'd look better in a Gatorade bottle. It's an alcohol thing.

CENTURY CLUB/GOLDEN ANNIVERSARY/POWER HOUR

The Truth: Remember when millions of people protested the invasion of Iraq in 2003? That was no protest; that was notoriously party-happy G-Dub organizing the largest Power Hour of all time under the clever ruse of sending troops (pouring beer) into Iraq (down our throats). But Congress, being the prudes they are, took him literally and began World War III. Talk about a drunken misunderstanding. . . .

Players: As many as possible

Supplies:
- A reliable person with a watch or a giant clock (Big Ben, for example)
- A shot glass per person

Beer: Eight to ten for each potential club member

Objective: To drink one hundred, fifty, or sixty shots of beer in as many minutes without puking. Seriously, that's it. Oh, and try not to bomb anybody.

Ticking Away: Not so much of a game as it is an event. People will organize Century Clubs and Power Hours by handing out fliers and posting notes on local community boards. There's even a world record for the Largest Power Hour as well as Most Consecutive Shots of Beer; look them up.

So, get everyone together in a big room, each person with his own shot glass and enough beer to fill it the desired number of times. When everybody's settled, the timer starts. Each time a minute passes, everybody takes down a shot of golden goodness. There are a few ways to keep track and count minutes:

- Whoever is the party master can type or write up a sheet with the numbers one to one hundred and have a clock sitting next to him, marking off the numbers as the clock changes. He is your drinking general for the night, but when he yells, "Drink!" you needn't ask, "How much, sir?" because you know, you know.
- There's actually a DVD you can buy called *Power Hour* that counts down minutes and makes you do funny shit like cartwheels and armpit farts and kissing your neighbor with a pussing-out penalty of, you bet: more shots of beer.
- You can program a cell phone, digital watch, or digital clock to have some kind of an alarm go off every minute, but this is outrageously annoying.
- If you use the music program iTunes, there is a feature that lets you choose sixty songs and it plays only the first minute of each selection so, when the song changes, you drink, and when the playlist is over, you have succeeded and can finally go pee.

Power Hour: By far the most popular "shot-of-beer-every-minute game" is Power Hour, which is sixty shots in sixty minutes. Perfect as a pre-funk because, if the football game starts at ten A.M., start at eight, so there's still plenty of time for face paint and chest bumps. It's nice because it's not too much for girls to drink, and the guys who play with them but don't want to leave to play Flip Cup just yet can just start the clock over for the highly prestigious Double Power Hour, and then spend the rest of the night trying to make a pyramid out of their empty beer cans.

Century Club: The Century Club is one hundred shots of beer in one hundred minutes and usually evokes one of two reactions:

1. "A hundred shots! Are you fucking kidding me?"
2. "That's it? You're talking beer, right?"

Both questions are easily answered:

1. "Yes, I'm sure a hundred shots of 4.2 percent Coors Light will make you deathly buzzed; relax, it's only ten beers max if you fill each shot to the brim."
2. "Tough guy, huh? Here, use this Milwaukee's Best Ice."

Golden Anniversary Club: The Golden Anniversary Club is for first-timers who usually have an ovary or two in their possession. Fifty shots in fifty minutes with either *Love Actually* or *My Best Friend's Wedding* playing in the background. Tissues are recommended.

Guys—Keira Knightley is primarily shown in the first fifty minutes of *Love Actually*. You're welcome.

Paragraph My Publisher Urged Me to Delete Due to Potential Lawsuits: There are two games played in Mexico, called the Dirty Dozen and the Filthy Fifteen. The first is twelve shots in twelve minutes; the second, fifteen shots in fifteen minutes—*of tequila.* However, due to FDA regulations and the fact that I don't want angry calls from your neighbor saying that I caused you to puke on her prized roses, I have to say that I do not recommend either of these games . . . but that they're really fun.

CRICKET

Australian Cricket World Cup: (commentary) *"The bloody wanker's only got a bickie of bees' knees for 'is yobbo ta bowl tha wickets. 'appy as a Larry wid 'is middys an' schooners. Best squib an onkus to save fair dinkum. The pitch . . . wowzing wallopers the ol' lirrkin's done it! The Roos win!"*

American Translation: The pitcher struck out the batter in the ninth inning.

Mates: Two teams of at least five blokes. The more, the better.

Supplies: A strong bladder

Tinny: A few slabs

Objective: For your team to score more points after the match. Oh, and men seem to appreciate this game more than women do. No offense, just saying.

Going Down Under: Buck's Night Out!

Decide who is on each team. This is very important because there's lots of rivalry and getting each other pumped up and excited and competitive and hammered and horny. Wait, scratch that last one.

Divide into two even teams unless Billy the Bladder is playing, because he counts as three large oxen. The team sits together and preferably out of earshot of its opponents so the teammates can discuss strategy. The object is to score points. You score one point for each beer your team drinks and you lose five points every time somebody takes a piss. There are no extra small beers, wine coolers, or any other mixed drinks, and tallboys (sixteen-ounce cans) still count as one.

The duration of the game is decided before you start, and is usually something like one or two hours, the length of a single movie, or some other measurable amount of time. Once the game begins, there is no leaving the room for any reason except to piss. If someone leaves for any other reason, his team loses five points just like a piss. Knowing this, take the amount of beers you think you can drink during the allotted time and add three (you'd be surprised what competitive drinking can do to you). Oh, and check the room beforehand to make sure no one hid any empty beer cans to add to their end-of-game total.

Each team can use a box, the floor, or whatever else it wants, to keep track of their beers. Each team should probably have its own kind of beer so the empty cans don't get mixed up. So, for example, the movie starts and everyone starts drinking. When someone finishes a can, he says, "Finished!" and tosses it into whatever his team is using to keep track. The other team must be able to see and easily count how many empty cans your team has at any given time, so its members can use strategy to pace themselves, catch up, or pass you. If you think it shouldn't be this way, think about this: in what sport can you *not* see the other team's score?

Make sure to keep track of the piss counts on paper or something that everyone can see. At the end of the allowed time or movie or whatever, you should already know who won, but count the empty beers minus the piss penalties anyway to declare the official winner.

If anybody pisses himself or gets sick (pukes/gives up), that player is eliminated from the game. His team isn't disqualified, but is down a player and loses five points because he "pissed off," as our Australian friends would say.

My Four Cents:

- Make sure to piss right before the game begins so you can wait the maximum amount of time before going.
- Nobody cheat and bring in already drunk cans. This is a gentleman's game (as you'll be lucky to find even one female who wants to play).

- Usually at the beginning and end of the game, there is heavy drinking by all players. This works but, in my experience, having certain people pound heavily at different times is better. Maybe have one or two guys drinking steadily the whole time, so there's a constant flow of empty cans coming from your side.
- Don't break your bladder.

Clever Australian Slang (that I didn't make up!):

Have a naughty: have sex
Off one's face: get drunk
Root: have sex
Have a session: get drunk
Crack a fat in a spunk: have sex
Gut full o' piss: get drunk

DRINK OR DARE

Trouble with the Family? Beer Can Help. See, beer is like a giant family that's constantly having family reunions in grocery stores and bars and my fridge. How do the relatives always get along? Simple: they keep a consistent blood alcohol content of between 3.9 and 8 percent. If we, as a family and as a species working as one for the betterment of humanity, *really* want to get along, we must strive for the same levels of alcoholism as displayed by the Beers family.

Players: The more diversified your group, the better, unless you're all supermodels, in which case there are no clothes allowed. Sorry—I don't make the rules. Oh wait, yes, I do—so you'd better listen.

Supplies:

- A brilliantly creative mind
- Ethics, morals, respect for the law
- The ability to look at the previous bullet point and laugh

Beer: Try something new, like instead of beer get "lots of beer." Diversity is key.

Objective: Don't puss out!

I Dare You to Read These Instructions: I'm assuming that everybody, even strict Mormons or Sri Lankan tribal warriors, knows how to play Truth or Dare. Anybody who has actually played it knows that the Truth option is about as fun as peeling your toenails off with a wrench. It's boring and, let's face it—no one cares how you feel about anything. Dares are where it's at, and the more alcohol and peer pressure involved, the better the dares get and the more likely people will actually do them. My game—Drink or Dare—is simply Truth or Dare but without the option of Truth.

Get as many people as you can into a room, preferably a mix of genders, and take turns asking someone to complete a dare of your choice. If you are in college, don't hold back. In high school, people would always have these wonderfully devious dares in mind but would never say them. Well, now's your chance. If someone won't do the dare or puts out a half-assed effort, he drinks fifteen. Yes, fifteen bigass gulps to drown away his inhibitions (a.k.a. fun destroyers). This is to encourage people to actually do the dares, or to at least get over-the-top drunk and *then* do the dares.

Before you embark on your journey of drunken debauchery, stomach butterflies, and racing hearts, let's take a moment to reflect on some outstandingly on-target words from a brilliant man, Mr. Mark Twain:

> Twenty years from now you will be more disappointed by the things that you didn't do than by the ones you did do. So throw off the bowlines. Sail away from the safe harbor. Catch the trade winds in your sails. Explore. Dream. Discover.
>
> **—Mark Twain, late 1800s**

What he's saying is "Do the dare, pussy." Do you really want to let Mark Twain down? Fine—how about this legendary quote:

> Twenty minutes from now, you'll be more disappointed by the cops that didn't chase you than by the ones that did. Throw off the chicken outfit. Sail away from the sober harbor! Catch the nighttime winds in your newly exposed loins! Explore the roof of Husky Stadium! Dream of running next to bouncing breasts! Discover what it's like to see yourself in the evening news and not remember it!
>
> **—Alex Bash, 2007**

DRINK

I Was Thinking . . . isn't it odd how when someone says, "I'm drinking tonight," he automatically means alcohol? What do nondrinkers say? Do they need to specify they are not drinking alcoholic beverages? I then realized this is an innate human quality. The fact that any sane and moderately educated person thinks "alcohol" when he hears "drinking" shows that we, as humans, have a predisposed inclination to consume alcohol. Now, be a good human and play this next game.

P-L-A-Y-E-R-S: Two to five works best.

S-U-P-P-L-I-E-S:

- Your average Oscar the Grouch–style garbage can

B-E-E-R: Plenty

O-B-J-E-C-T-I-V-E: To make the other players get D-R-I-N-K before you do

B-A-S-I-C-S: I'm assuming you all know how to play the basketball game Horse, but if not, here goes. Players take turns taking shots. If Player One makes his shot, Player Two needs to shoot and make the same one, or he gets the letter H. If Player Two makes it, then Player Three has to make the same shot; if he misses, he gets H. You get letters in the order of H-O-R-S-E. When you get HORSE, you lose.

DRINK works the same way but with empty beer cans for basketballs and a garbage can or recycling bin for a hoop. Players take turns shooting their empty beer cans into the trash/recycling bin from wherever, and however they like. You can play in a room full of obstacles or outside in some yard or anyplace else your drunken heart desires (yes, hearts get drunk; why else would girls cry all the time?).

Here's the catch: you can only take your shot when you finish a beer so, as you can see through your bloodshot eyes, the game moves slightly slower than Horse. Each player can bring a maximum of three empty beer cans to the game, so everyone can start playing right away.

Decide the order you're going to play in. Make sure if you choose to go first, that you can keep up drink-wise, because you only have seven minutes to finish each beer. You can stockpile empty ones if you're a champion drinker and save them for future shots, but you still need to allow each player the allotted seven minutes' drinking time between shots. If you finish a beer, take your shot, and miss it, you get to keep that beer for your next turn. Don't complain, tough guys: if you discarded the can each shot regardless of whether you missed or made it, you'd drink thirty beers a game.

Each.

If Player One finishes his beer and makes his shot from, say, the top of a chair while standing on one foot, Player Two then needs to take his empty can and make the same shot, or he gets a D. When you get D-R-I-N-K, you are out; last player left wins.

O-T-H-E-R- I-S-H:

- When you have D-R-I-N and you miss a shot you were supposed to make, you can either choose to "chance it" and take one more shot to try to make it, thus not getting the K, or you can make the player who shot the original shot "prove it" and make it again. For these shots, you can use the same beer you originally sank.

- It's up to you to either leave the can fully composed or crush it before you shoot. Different techniques may work better for different shots.

- If it takes too long for people to finish their beer, try playing on teams taking turns shooting, but drink together so you have a constant flow of projectiles.

- Get creative. Just as in real HORSE, playing with regular shots gets old. Try shooting backward, using your feet, around the back, take off clothing, sacrificing your firstborn etc.

Wise Advice of DRINK: **D**on't **R**un **IN**to **K**nives, **D**o **R**ejoice **IN** **K**eyStone

I'VE NEVER

Drunk Court: There needs to be a Court for Drunken Crimes when people wake up and apparently, for example, had peed on the police chief's unwilling daughter. Evidence could be an empty pint of Turkey with the assailant's fingerprints, shotgunned beers with personalized knife holes, or a tournament of Beer Pong so massive only he could have organized it. Prosecutors would reference the thirteen urine samples recovered on the way to the crime scene. Every case would end with the judge saying, "Major party foul; seriously, bro, not cool."

Players: A good game should have no less than six, at least two of which should be sheltered country girls, crack dealers, or the late Evel Knievel.

Supplies: To have ten fingers. Sorry, lawn-mower-accident-Joey.

Beer: Unless you're that boy-in-the-bubble kid, probably a lot

Objective: To be the last one with fingers remaining . . . or the first to lose them

Court Is Now in Session: Everybody hangs out with all ten fingers raised up in front of his chest as if he was going to double high-five somebody. Or slap someone in the boobs.

Take turns going around the circle saying things that you haven't done. This can be anything from, "I've never ridden in an airplane" to "I've never smoked weed" to "I've never had sex in a baseball field." Get as crazy as you like.

If someone says on his turn that he's never done something and you *have* done that activity, you put down a finger. So if you've been skydiving before, and Susie-Q says on her turn, "I've never gone skydiving," you'd put down a finger. Every time you put down a finger, you drink two. When you put down your final finger, you are out, and also get the pleasure of drinking ten more for losing (or winning; however you want to look at it).

I'll Hold You in Contempt! (Drunk Tank):

- If you're scared about skeletons in your closet being exposed, don't play this game. If you literally have skeletons in your closet, find a better hiding place.
- If you've actually done something that nobody else has, don't lie and be like, "Yeah, me neither, who would do *that*!?" Just admit it and put down a finger, you whore.
- Don't single somebody out. If you know someone is a twin (like me), don't be that douche bag who says, "I've never been in the womb with somebody else, ha ha." This is lame, and keep this in mind: there are two of us, and we are bigger than you.
- Also, there's no "I've never had a penis" or "I've never had fallopian tubes." Yeah, none of that shit.

On a Side Note: A pig's orgasm can last for thirty minutes. This is why bacon tastes so good and why we shouldn't feel bad about eating pigs: they've lived well enough. Oh, and in case you were wondering, "fallopian tube" makes a great insult.

OUT THE WAZOO

Nominal Aphasia: a temporary affliction where someone gets so drunk he can't piece together proper sentences. I came down with it one evening and my bastard friends found it funny that I made no sense and took delight in trying to remember the random string of concepts I was spewing, drinking each time they messed up. This is how this game was created, and also explains why three of them have gone missing.

Players: Two or more

Supplies: A decent memory

Beer Holder: You can chug faster out of a glass

Objective: To remember every item that's been said

Entering the Wazoo: Very simple: You sit around in a circle and take turns saying a word. This word can be a noun, verb, adjective, place, theory, country, whatever. It can also be a two-word concept, like "dude sauce." It also doesn't really have to make sense, like "poop wave" or "advanced calculus."

So, on your turn, you say, "Boat." Damn, you are boring. The next player has to say, "Boat" and then a word of his own, like "quantum physics." The next player (and it could be Player One again) has to say, "Boat, quantum physics," and then, I dunno, "Sri Lanka." The next player says, "Boat, quantum physics, Sri Lanka," and then his own word. This goes on around the circle until somebody messes up. This person drinks two for each word that needed to be remembered, including the one he fucked up on. So if he got the first six words but couldn't recall "trigonometric meat sance," he'd drink fourteen. Each person only has five seconds to think of the item before it counts as messing up.

Pulling Out of the Wazoo:

- Try playing in Spanish. If someone doesn't know Spanish, well, he'll be drinking a lot.
- Try having to go in alphabetical order; it'll make it easier to remember each one and therefore people will drink more when they mess up.

- Try playing where all the items have to relate to a particular category, like cars, beer companies, vegetables, famous people, things to throw at Delta Upsilon from the alley, etc.

Out the Wazoo Definition: "in excessive amounts," also "anus."

Dear Parents: Studies have shown that students learn best when they study in a comfortable, natural environment similar to the one in which they carry out their everyday lifestyle. Therefore, if you really want your child to do well in college, start him on a steady diet of Out the Wazoo at a young age so, by the time he reaches college and is drinking heavily anyway, he will be in his natural studying habit! Dean's list, here we come!

PILLARS

The Great Chicken Conspiracy: After launching the most successful marketing campaign of all time with the slogan "Tastes like Chicken," chickens have moved one step closer to taking over the world. With ranks topping twenty-four billion, they could attack with nearly four chickens to every one human. Four chickens couldn't kill a human, you say? What about specially trained combat chickens? Better play this next game to numb the nightmares you're now having.

Players: Two or four

Supplies:

- A rectangular table
- One Ping-Pong ball
- The ability to run around frantically

Beer: Full, unopened cans; no cups

Objective: To finish your beers first

Attacking the Coop: Usually teams of one or two work best, but three people per team works, too. We're going to use an example with two teams of two (four players total). Teams take sides on the short ends of the rectangular table. Each player sets down an unopened beer in front of him at his corner of the table. Whichever team's combined boob size is the biggest goes first and, yes, if it's all guys playing, then boob size still determines the first turn.

Teams take turns throwing the Ping-Pong ball at the other team's beer cans. If the ball touches either of the beer cans in any way, the team that threw opens its beers and starts to chug. The players continue chugging as fast as they can until the other team has grabbed the ball and slammed it back onto the table and yelled, "Stop!" The object is to finish your beers first, so obviously the object is to throw the Ping-Pong ball as hard and as accurately as you can at the other team's beers and drink as fast as you can.

Players cannot protect or block their cans in any way. If the other team does block its beer or interfere with the throw, the throwing players get to drink for two seconds and get the ball back. There's only one Ping-Pong ball, so players on each team take turns throwing.

Fending the Foul:

- Don't be a douche bag and drink for longer than you should. As soon as you hear or see them slam the ball down to the table or yell, "Stop," cease drinking immediately.

- If you throw the ball at the can and it bounces back toward you, don't block it or swipe at it or anything. If it does hit you, just stand there and keep drinking.

- If one player finishes drinking before the other (this usually happens), the first person done keeps playing by throwing and retrieving the ball and whatnot, but just doesn't drink.

- If someone "accidentally" knocks over his beer and spills some, the other team gets to drink for two seconds as a penalty.
- When you throw the ball you can*not* lean over the table or "break the invisible plane" at each of the table's ends. Basically, your hand or arm cannot go above the table when you throw.

For Your Inebriated Consideration:

- If the ball goes bouncing really far away, it's totally fine (and a good idea) to have one guy wait by the table and have the other player throw it back to him. Keep in mind a Ping-Pong ball does not fly like a baseball, and throwing and catching is not especially easy when drunk.
- Harder throws may not always be better. Softer and better-aimed throws can be a game-ender if you make them bounce off down the road.
- You can view it as a challenge or a major annoyance to play this game in a crowded room.
- Yes, each player can start the game with two unopened cans if he is so inclined. Thanks for asking.

RUGBY

Four simple steps to making a live sporting event more fun:

1. Drink heavily and continue to do so upon arriving at the stadium.
2. Insult people undeserving of verbal attack, such as grandparents and anybody who isn't you.

3. Tell them to go fuck themselves when they politely ask you to refrain from cursing because there are children present.

4. Borrow girlfriend's makeup to cover up your black eye.

Players: A group of five to eight guys works best

Supplies:
- A round table to sit at or the ability to stand in a circle (very rare)
- Coordination

Beer: True rugby players have no limit

Objective: To not mess up and make awesome motion-represented tackles

Scrum for Life: Everybody sits or stands in a circle. The game is played with an imaginary rugby ball. Yes, imaginary—there is no ball. Whoever has the ball pretends he is holding it. Somebody catches the fake rugby ball from the fake punt and has several fake options:

- To pass it to the left, he raises his left elbow.
- To pass it right, he raises his right elbow.
- To pass it two players to the left, he pats his left shoulder with his right hand.
- To pass it two players to the right, he pats his right shoulder with his left hand.
- To pass it directly across, he extends both arms and points directly at that person.

Whoever was passed the ball has the same options as above.

Most important part of the game: When somebody has the ball, players can tackle him (not literally . . . Well, or literally). To tackle somebody, you have to hit your left shoulder with your right hand and then your right shoulder with your left hand, repeat, and then throw both hands toward the person with the ball before he can successfully pass it away.

The tackling process should take two or three seconds, so when you get the ball you'd better move fast. It's up to the majority of players who weren't involved in the tackling process to decide if the player with the ball passed it off in time. They also have to decide if the tackler actually went through the tackling process correctly and didn't just wave his arms around and throw them out like one of those crazy inflatable wavy arm thingys at used car lots. You know what I'm talking about.

- If you get tackled, you drink five.
- If you tackle someone who never even had the ball, drink three. Nice try.
- If you make an ambiguous pass and no one knows what the fuck you meant, drink two.
- If you think the ball got passed to you but it really didn't and you make a passing move, drink two.
- If the ball *did* get passed to you and you don't notice or "catch it," drink two.

The Manliness Calculator: Anybody notice how the manlier a sport is (rugby, football, hockey, boxing), the more likely the spectators will be thoroughly intoxicated? Like, shit-faced-drunk-and-rowdy intoxicated? Well, I created a manliness-to-drunkenness equation to calculate the level of intoxication of the crowd with regard to the physical action of the sport's participants.

$$[(X + Y + Z) \times Q - P] \div F = \text{drunkenness}$$

X: Number of physical contacts you can hear from the stands (tackles, checks, punches, snapping bones, etc.)
Y: Mad balls-out dashes toward a player to inflict harm (chasing a wide receiver, tracking down a forward, advancing on your opponent, etc.)
Z: Instances where it's completely legal to inflict pain upon another player (punch, tackle, impale, etc.)
Q: Number of fights that spontaneously break out
P: Minutes of game delay due to penalties, fouls, or injuries
F: Number of well-known female players

THE NAME GAME

What was the preferred sex position of the Renaissance? Well, in the Renaissance, people didn't believe they had sexual identities, instead viewing sex as an art. Today we call this being out-of-your-fucking-mind crazy, or porn. As the inventers of porn, the Renaissance is responsible for the Swedish Midget+Billy Goat Gang Bang, their unanimous favorite position.

Players: Two or more, best with eight or so (one being the goat, of course)

Supplies: One vocal chord for each player

Beer: Beer

Objective: To quickly think of unnamed famous people

Arranging the Midgets: Everybody sits around in at least somewhat of a circle; seats of a car or sprawled out couches will do. The person with the biggest earlobes goes first (you *must* measure). Player One says the first and last name of a famous person, such as Michael Jordan. Player Two then has to say the name of another famous person whose first name starts with the first letter of the first famous person's last name. Confused? It's simple, I'll show you.

Player One: Michael **J**ordan,
Player Two: **J**ulius **E**rving,
Player Three: **E**dward **N**orton
Player Four: **N**aomi **W**atts
Player Five: **W**inston **C**hurchill, etc.

Look easy enough? Good: two more things. If someone comes up whose first and last names start with the same letter (**J**anet **J**ackson) or someone with only one name (Jesus, Madonna), the rotation switches. For example (watch the Player One, Two, Three, etc.):

Player One: Barry **M**anilow
Player Two: **M**ichael **J**ordan
Player Three: **J**anet **J**ackson
Player Two: **J**ames **D**ean
Player One: **D**avy Crockett, etc.

You Drink 5 Drinks When:

- You can't think of one fast enough (three to five seconds).
- Mess up on the letter matchup. This can be from using the first letter of the *first* name instead of the *last* name, or if you suck at spelling and think that Ford has a silent *q*.
- If you say one that's already been said (pay attention, drunky!)
- You use a nickname when the real name is widely known (Shaquille O'Neill's name isn't Shaq).
- If you are a famous person and you say your own name, you are a conceited dick and must finish every drink that's currently

within a ten-foot radius of your gigantic head. Unless your name is Samuel Adams, because that is just awesome.

Note: Some people call this game Harmon Killebrew. This is lame. Yes, his last name is almost "kill a brew." We get it. Very clever. Also, that "really popular guy" from high school is not famous and your girlfriend is not "almost a famous model." Drink up.

THUMPER!

Words of Wisdom: When hanging out drinking with the boys, a mass streaking or mooning sounds like a fun idea. That is, until you're all standing there awkwardly with your asses hanging out, waiting for the mooning victim to walk by, or you become aware of the uncomfortable pseudo-gayness of the initial strip-down before the streaking. For these reasons, either involve a high ratio of females or drink five extra beers for each bare male ass.

Players! Five to ten!!!

Supplies!
- Loving to yell and pound on things!
- A fucking table!

Beer! Fuck-loads! AAAAHHHH!

Objective! To pound, yell, and fucking drink! Fuck, yeah!

Basics, Motherfucker! Before the game starts, everybody has to pick a motion that will represent him. These are usually sexual, derogatory, or embarrassing to somebody, but can also be random. For example, your motion could be waving your hands in the air, doing a mock bench press, pulling on your ears, or giving a fake blow job. Make sure everybody knows everyone else's motions. All players then sit around the table and start to pound on it as hard and fast as they can with both palms.

Somebody (whoever wants to) yells out:

Yelling Guy: "What's this game called!?"
Everybody else: "Thumper!"
Yelling Guy: "Why do we play it!?"
Everybody else: "To get fucked up!"
Yelling Guy: "WHY DO WE PLAY IT!?"
Everybody else: "TO GET FUCKED UP!"

After the yelling stops, you must continue thumping but not as hard as before, so that you don't want to quit playing in two minutes when your hands start to bleed. But, if you want to, it's always encouraged—in Thumper it's always okay to pound and yell. The Yelling Guy does his motion for about three seconds and then immediately transfers into doing somebody else's motion. Everybody has to be watching because if he starts doing *your* motion, you'd better be ready to start doing your motion for about three seconds before then transferring into somebody else's. The funnier your motions are the more fun it'll be, especially if someone is shy or quiet and has to act as if he's fellating a goat or something.

If that's confusing, picture this: there are four guys playing, JV, Spot, Alex, and Randy McCheese Whiz. Our symbols, for the sake of easiness are:

JV:	clapping
Spot:	snapping
Alex:	patting his head
Randy McCheese Whiz:	waving his hands around like a drunken uncoordinated baseball fan on camera

Alex yells the Thumper Intro and starts patting his head, then after a few seconds he starts snapping. Spot must immediately start snapping, then after a few seconds he could start clapping. JV then starts clapping for a few moments and then starts waving his hands around like an idiot, which makes Randy McCheese Whiz start to wave *his* hands around like an idiot, and so on. It may sound like a brain-damaged caveman created this game (entirely possible) but it's really fun.

Very important: There is no just *saying*, "Thumper." "Thumper" must always be yelled as if you were ten beers drunker than you really are. And, when writing out the word, you must always add an exclamation point, unless of course you are explaining how to play and write the word *Thumper!*

As if yelling and shouting and pounding aren't enough, here's how you drink:

- If you mess up on doing somebody else's motion or do a half-assed job of it, you drink three and should probably laugh along with everybody else laughing at you.
- If you don't realize that the motion got passed to you, drink three.
- If you do a motion that no one recognizes, drink three. This happens.
- If somebody ever says something about Thumper! without yelling it or pounding on something as they says it, they drink three. This is the essence of Thumper!

A Quick Word from Thumper: THUMPER!!!!! FUCK YOU!!!! GET FUCKED UP!!!! OVERUTILIZE EXCLAMATION POINTS!!!!! THUMPER!! FUCK YEEEEAAAAHHH!!!

WORDS OF THE NIGHT

Improving Communication: There are two major grammatical changes in the English language that only emerge after a double-digit number of drinks have been consumed. The first is the elimination of spaces between words, which is of course pragmatic because we can communicate quicker. The second is that formalities and niceties are very well pronounced, sometimes used several times before anything is actually said, as in, "Hey, Alex; bro; dude; hey, man; Bash; listen to this, bro; so I was . . ."

Players of the Morning: Everybody

Supplies of the Afternoon: Nada

Beer of the Evening: Have some with you at all times

Objective of the Night: To not say "the words of the night"

Basics of the Darkness: Before they start drinking, each of the players has to pick two nouns. These can be anything from *house* to *Costa Rica* to *dog* to *herpes.* Whatever you want. For the remainder of the night, whenever any of the nouns are spoken by anybody, those playing drink one. And when I say anybody, I *mean* anybody. On TV, the radio, a random passerby, someone on the phone, from the plant after dropping LSD, etc. If the words are *ever* uttered, those playing drink one.

Suggestions of the Early Morning Hours:

- It is fun to play this while playing other drinking games, to add to the number of times people yell, "Oooohhhh!!" and "Drink!"

- Try restricting all the nouns to a certain category, such as drinking nouns. This way, the nouns are more recognizable and could potentially make you drink a lot more. Hooray!
- If you want to be a bitch, choose a noun like *thunder* and then lock some guys in a room while blaring AC/DC's *Thunderstruck*. Wear earplugs and make sure they're honorable.
- Somebody, please, for the sake of stories you won't want to tell your children, pick the words *the* and *a*.

Suggestions of the Couch You Woke Up On: There's a reason this game is right before the Movie Games section (besides the fact it starts with *w* and is last in alphabetic order). Words of the Night is a perfect game to play while watching a movie like *Casino*, so you can pick the word *fuck* and drink 398 times.

MOVIE GAMES!!

LORD OF THE RINGS TRILOGY

Bilbo's *Real* Poem:

All that is beer does not glitter; not all who pass out get tossed,
Good beers can come before liquor; dicks look good drawn in lip gloss.
From keg stands a champ will be woken, slurs from his drunk mind shall spring,
Renewed shall be hookups once broken, praise for tequila he'll sing!

Players: If you come from somewhere that begins with "University of . . ." or ends in ". . . University" or ". . . College," you should be good to go. Unemployed recovering alcoholics are also welcome.

Supplies:

- An incredible attention span
- A giant TV and DVD player
- A golden ring that whispers creepily to you
- Hairy feet

Grog: The Shire's Best Lite

Location: The Land of Middle-earth . . . so yes, your parents' basement.

Objective: To defeat Sauron! Or at least penetrate that suspiciously vaginal-looking eye of his (wear a condom).

Beginning the Quest: Real champions play this game by watching all three films *in a row*. They also sometimes slip into a coma around the battle of Helm's Deep, but who's counting? So, call some girls over and . . . ha! Just kidding. Grab your male companions and get to work; I suggest starting at noon.

How to Drink in Middle-earth:

- Pick a character; each time this person kills somebody, drink one.
- Every time there's homosexual tension between Frodo and Sam, drink one. Each time Sam says, "Oh, Mr. Frodo . . ." drink five.
- Every time a character drinks, drink one. If it's a hobbit, drink two. If it's Aragorn, get all tingly inside and drink three. If it's Gimli, drink four and have a burping contest. If it's Legolas, go wash your hair—there's no time for drinking. Lather, rinse, and repeat!
- Each time one of the main characters uses his species' special talent, drink one (Legolas = sight, Aragorn = tracking, Gimli = being short, Hobbits = being short, Orcs = grunting, Wizards = growing exceptionally long hair).
- Each time Legolas's blond locks look especially good, drink 0.1. Any more and you'd pass out in minutes.
- Each time you wonder, "Who knew they had bad English accents in Middle-earth?" drink one.
- Each time Peter Jackson was totally going for an Oscar, drink one (awe-inspiring speech, overly dramatic camera shot obviously from helicopter, weird artsy music accompanied by slow-motion montage, large bribe to the academy, etc.).

- Each time Aragorn argues with someone and is obviously right, get sweaty palms and drink three.
- Each time someone looks angst-ridden, drink one. If it's Legolas, swoon and drink two more. If it's Sauron, lay off the shrooms: he's a burning oval; there is nothing but angst.
- Every time a Nazgul screams, drink 1 and recommend Vicks VapoRub. Hold an irritating noise contest.
- Every time a player sings or hums along to one of the Middle-earth songs jump-kick him in the larynx and pour two drinks in his eyes, one of which dribbles down into his mouth.
- Every time a character draws a sword more slowly and cinematically than it's pragmatic to do in the heat of battle, drink two. Axes and wands count, too.
- When Frodo's eyes roll back in his head, drink one and comment on how you wish you had *those* drugs.
- Every time Elrond looks overly elfish, drink two and say, "Did you guys know he's Agent Smith in the *Matrix* movies?"
- Drink one each time someone is smoking. Five drinks for each smoke ship they send sailing through a smoke ring. Wonder how much of the journey is just hallucinations.
- Every time Gollum spazzes out and gets all schizo on us, drink one. *Schizo* being defined as "an act or statement that can't be justified no matter the level of intoxication."
- Each time Gimli is the comic relief, drink one. If you actually laugh, stop drinking—you've had enough.
- Each time a movie ends, drink ten and talk about how awesome it was. Polish your golden shrine to Aragorn. Orc porn isn't out of the question.

- Each time one of your buddies begins a sentence with, "Wait, couldn't they have just . . . ?" slap him and force five drinks down his throat. Nobody questions Peter Jackson!
- Every time the fellowship of the ring treacherously overcome a treacherous treachery, drink one and cheer in whatever Middle-earth tongue you'd like.
- Each time someone is beheaded, drink ten and eye your neighbor's dinner knife suspiciously.
- Each time Aragorn saves Frodo's life as only Aragorn can, look into his deep blue eyes and faint. When you come to, drink three.
- When the final credits roll, cry because it's over, cry because you made it, and cry because you probably pissed yourself for the fourth time in the last nine hours.

LORD OF THE RINGS TRILOGY: THE REMIX

(Choosing to Drink by Character Only)

Frodo (The shortest player):

- When he bitches about wanting to go home, drink one and remind him he'll get way more poon-tang if he saves the world.
- Drink two whenever he actually fights; remind him that Spud Webb was only five foot six and *he* won a dunk contest. Saving Middle-earth is like a lay-up.
- Drink one whenever he almost dies. Hope you don't get called in to work the next morning.

- Drink one every time he stupidly trusts Gollum when he probably should have just slit his throat but couldn't because Peter Jackson wanted to make documentaries about how they made Gollum look so real.

- If Frodo ever needs a hug, consume 0.01 drinks. Get at least an eighteen-pack for this.

- Whenever Frodo could have easily been raped by Sam, drink one.

- Each time Frodo saves the world, finish your drink.

Sam (The fattest player):

- Whenever Sam has to encourage Frodo to carry on, drink two. Each time Frodo responds with, "You try carrying this fucking ring, Shamu!" drink ten.

- Each time Sam is a Shire-obsessed pussy, drink 2.

- Every time he complains about hunger, remind him that Sauron sprayed pesticide and the crops are no longer certified organic. Oh, and drink two.

- Each time Sam throws himself pitifully into battle, drink two and tell him he'd be better off just giving hand jobs to relieve stress.

- Whenever Sam gets frustrated because his forceful penetration of Mr. Frodo's weakened behind gets interrupted by a giant spider or ring wraith, drink three.

- Whenever Sam is the least important character in the scene, drink 0.25 drinks. A fifth of something nice should do for this rule.

- Waterfall the entire time Sam is carrying Frodo. If a fat little hobbit can carry someone after venturing to Mount Doom, you can pound a beer or two. Selfish bastard . . .

Aragorn (The most outrageously good-looking player [decided by female]):

- Whenever Aragorn is "the Man," drink one. (Note: He is *always* the Man.)

- Each time he saves someone's life who was for sure going to get jacked-the-fuck-up, drink three and hide your boner in the elastic band of your shorts (Note: Wear shorts with elastic band if playing as Aragorn).

- Each time he and Frodo have a special moment together, drink two. (Note: Every moment with Aragorn is special.)

- When someone calls him anything other than Aragorn (Strider, the King, Ranger, Horse Cock, etc.), drink three. (Note: Hold back from calling Aragorn "Baby Cakes" until in private; some consider this "gay.")

- Whenever he kills somebody, drink one. (Note: If Aragorn's blade even grazes your skin, you go into anaphylactic shock.)

- Whenever he uses his pimp ranger skills, drink two. (Note: looking great is a skill of rangers.)

- If he is ever crowned king, drink ten and end your life: it will never be as good as it is right now.

Gimli (The hairiest player):

- Whenever he is the comic relief, drink two and laughingly spew all over whoever is playing as Legolas (see below).

- Every time he axes a bitch, drink one. Awesome.

- Every time he is pitifully in the shadow of Legolas, drink two and remind him that his mommy still thinks he's handsome.

- Every time he rides horseback behind someone else, drink two and send him his disabilities check.

- Each time Gimli's beard should have fallen out of its braids but didn't, drink two.
- For each ax he pulls out of his ass after throwing the first one, drink three.
- Every time he takes pride in being a midget with overproductive hair growth hormones, drink three.

Legolas (Player with longest hair):

- Drink two every time Gimli is the comic relief and smack him in the face before he can spew beer all over you (see above).
- Each time his hair looks especially amazing, drink 0.5 and pull your hat down a little farther.
- Each time you find yourself wondering how or when he conditions his hair amid the worldwide turmoil, drink two. Drink ten if you see him washing out the Head & Shoulders.
- When he speaks in Elfish, drink three and imitate Dave Chapelle saying, "I can't understand you, go back to your country . . . elf power." If you don't know what I'm talking about, drink three and pay more attention to life.
- When you mistake Legolas for a bangin' hot girl (or mistake a bangin' hot girl for Legolas), drink two and keep your mouth shut.
- Whenever he says something that makes absolutely no fucking sense, like, "The stars are cloaked in a mysterious veil," and everyone just stands there like, "Thanks for the tip, douche bag," drink five.
- Every time he kills someone, drink one and stare smugly at whoever is playing as Gimli.
- Each time Legolas misses a shot with his bow and arrow, drink eighteen billion.

Gandalf (Oldest player):

- Each time Gandalf could have made things a whole lot easier by using his magic and not running off to do wizard shit, drink two.
- Each time he casts a spell, drink two. Each time he should have cast another spell and not just stood there all stoic, drink another two.
- Drink three every time he says something abstract that no one without a three-foot beard would understand.
- When he and Frodo have a "moment," drink three and wonder who's going to eventually land Frodo in the sack.
- Whenever he is called something other than Gandalf (Gandalf the Grey, the White Wizard, Ian McKellan, etc.) drink five.
- Each time Gandalf does indeed kick some serious ass, drink three.
- If Gandalf gets something back in his possession without explanation (his hat, staff, horse), drink four and rap, "Damn it feels good to be a Gandalf."

Mary/Pippin (Most annoying player [decided by general consensus]):

- Each time they are total fucking pussies, drink one.
- Each time one or the other's voice noticeably squeaks, drink two.
- Each time they make enormous amounts of trouble for the fellowship and really shouldn't have even come, drink two.
- If one of them cries, start quoting Rambo and Terminator to deflect the pussiness and drink five to numb your emotions.

- If one of them is shown alone, drink one and sing your favorite song that has to do with being lonely.
- If either one talks about food, point out that alcohol has calories and drink three.
- Each time their smile want you to drop-kick them, drink 0.5.

Gollum (Skinniest, player):

- Each time Gollum is more than fifteen meters away from Frodo (they use the metric system in Middle-earth), drink three.
- Each time he says, "Gollum," in that disgusting coughlike fashion, drink one and FedEx some throat lozenges.
- Each time he eats something, drink two and direct him to the food pyramid.
- If you ever wonder what his penis looks like, drink three and be ashamed of yourself.
- "Precious . . . ," drink 1.
- Each time he uses improper grammar by adding an *s* onto the end of something, drink one.
- Each time you find Gollum attractive, see a counselor. Don't even drink.
- Each time Gollum melts in a fiery inferno, drink ten.

5 Questions for the LOTR Crew:

1. Ring Wraiths = the gothic emo kids of Middle-earth? Anyone?
2. Couldn't Frodo have just ridden Gandalf's eagle to Mount Doom and dropped in the ring and spared thousands of lives and the near-collapse of the entire world?
3. Honestly, did Gollum really get the recommended intake of calcium and zinc?

4. If Gandalf really is the most powerful wizard, then can he make his, um, you know, *bigger*?

5. Just come out of the closet, Sam. Seriously. You're not fooling anyone.

SCARFACE

Parents: If you think your son is considering the cocaine-trafficking business, remind him that if he chooses that route, he'll probably get pumped full of lead by a team of ruthless assassins and bleed to death in some godforsaken pool in Colombia. Then, put him back in his crib.

Players: Say hello to some little friends. Or regular-size friends; I don't discriminate, unless they are exceptionally large friends and carry grenade launchers.

Supplies: (Original supplies being held by FBI)

Beer: *¡Mucha Cerveza!*

Objective: Try to not bury your face in a salad bowl of coke.

Trafficking 101: Fucking pop in the fucking flick and for fuck's sake make sure no fucking kids are in hearing distance. *Scarface* is a fucking fuckload of a fan-fucking-tastic film, but I don't fucking want any fucking kids hearing all the "naughty words" and starting to fucking cuss all the fucking time.

Rule: Drink one when you hear the word *Fuck.*

WEDDING CRASHERS

Rules of Bar Crashing:

Rule #5: *The only thing that should come between you and a fellow Bar Crasher is a female's breast, which must at least be perky C's.*

Rule #17: *Every female who goes out deserves the chance to put out. Don't deny her this right.*

Rule #58: *If she doesn't like something you're wearing, you lost a bet.*

Crashers: Single people with no desire to settle down who want to sleep with other single people with no desire to settle down until they are no longer single and decide to settle down

Supplies:

- Fake awesome-sounding names
- Fake professions that nobody in the world actually has (lead Ferrari buyer, orgasm practitioner, skyscraper climber, successful day trader, etc.)

Drink: Champagne, bitches! Time to celebrate watching other people celebrate!

Bar-Crashing Rule #19: *Give loud toasts to events that are not taking place. If a fellow Bar Crasher is in need, toast to his twenty-eighth birthday, just like you did last week for someone else. And remember: it's never the wrong time for a "Salute our Troops" speech.*

Pre-funking the Wedding:

- Whenever a rule is mentioned, drink two, unless it's the one about, "Only have one strong drink or two beers." In this case, have one strong drink or two beers.

- When the infamous "Chaz" is mentioned, yell about meat loaf and drink three. Smack whoever starts doing his favorite Will Ferrell impressions (this will happen).

Bar Crashing Rule #39: *A way to a women's vagina is through tequila.*

- Really want to live in a movie? Drink one drink every time someone on the screen drinks.

Bar Crashing Rule #74: *In case of emergency, order Jager bombs.*

- Each time Jeremy (Vince Vaughn) speaks hilariously fast, drink three.
- Each time John's (Owen Wilson) voice sounds especially whiny, drink two and wish your soft, high voice could pull that many girls.
- Each time a different wedding is shown, drink two.

Bar Crashing Rule #86: *Tightness of shirt says a lot about the man.*

- Each time "the Sack" is a douche bag, drink one in the taxi ride home, and then again on the floor when you get back.
- Each time Grandma Cleary says something you wish you could get away with, drink 1.

Bar Crashing Rule #25: *It was always an inside joke between you and a friend; you didn't mean it that way.*

- Drink one for each bite or mentioning of finger foods and appetizers. Crab cakes count as two, obviously.
- Each time John calls Jeremy a name other then "Jeremy," drink one. If anyone can say, "Baba ghanoush," exactly in line with the movie without rewinding, he gets to hand out ten drinks.

Bar Crashing Rule #35: *Fuck breakfast.*

- Each time Todd is creepy, drink two and call whoever of your friends most resembles him "Todd." He will love this. Drink one each time he says, "Seriously, stop calling me that . . ."
- Most important: For each boob, drink one.

Bar Crashing Rule #37: *Drink as much as you like. The beauty of Bar Crashing is, if you get too drunk to properly close an attractive deal, you'll move on to less-attractive deals and not give a fuck.*

Happy Crashing!!!

BEERFEST

Hold Your Own Beerfest (American Style): You'll need light, low-carb beer and finger foods. If everyone is white, play hip-hop. No one dance. Have breaks every twenty minutes to check the Dow Jones. Bomb somebody. Brag about your dad's salary. Hug the toilet. Piss the bed. Blame the dog.

Improving Your Beerfest: Watch this movie, play this game.

Festival-Goers: Really though, this game is for heavy drinkers only (read: get your little brother *completely shit-housed*).

Festival Supplies: The ability to let your mind slip into a state of what some call "stupid fucking moronism." This allows to you (a) laugh at dumb shit, (b) shout loud, slurred jokes that no one understands but laughs at anyway, and (c) laugh at loud, slurred jokes.

Festival Fuel: Beer you can cheer and don't mind getting slopped all over you.

Objective: *Um den Esel von jedem zu treten, und um die Bierfeier zu gewinnen!* (Translation: "Win.")

Lassen Sie dem Bier fest beginnt! (Translation: "Go.")

- Each time someone in the movie says, "Wolfhausen," shout it back at him, cheers your beers, and drink two.
- Each time someone in the movie burps, burp loudly back at him, cheers your beers, and drink two.
- Each time someone calls Gam-Gam a whore, shout it back at him, cheers your beers, and drink two.
- When a member of the German team says some douche-bag comment about America blowing ass at drinking, shout it back at him, cheers your beers, and drink two.
- Each time someone mentions Fink's being a Jew or Todd's screwing Barry's wife, shout the comment back at the screen, cheers your beers, and drink two.
- Each time someone says, "Schnitzengiggle," quietly repeat it to yourself while chuckling, shake your friend's hand, and sip two little gulps.

Continued Education: The average American drinks 230 beers each year, placing us thirteenth in beer consumption per capita. This is pathetic. I know a guy who drank 150 beers in seventy-two hours. Seriously. Even Finland is laughing at us, and they don't even have nukes. They're barely even a country and they drink more than we do. Sure, we live in opulence, but what good is money if you don't blow it on booze?!

Master's Program: Watch this movie, play this game, and double all drinks. We'll be climbing the list in no time.

BEERFEST: THE REMIX

Disclaimer: I am not liable for: drunk dials, bruises, lost credit cards, torn clothing, severed limbs, felony charges, taxi rides home from the next state over, doctor's bills, future unemployment, blackmail, divorce settlements, estranged family members, ~~death~~ painful resurrection, or the sniffles (can't all be dramatic).

Players: Suicidal alcoholics

Supplies:
- Lack thereof "the will to live"
- A defibrillator (if you change your mind about the last bullet point)

Beer: Belgium. You will need all the beer in Belgium.

Objective: Maintain major organ function. If you do this, you will have succeeded.

Rule: Each time someone drinks, drink one. Two people drinking means two drinks, four people drinking means four drinks, and so on.

Disclaimer #2: I am 100 percent liable for: lottery tickets purchased while blacked out, incredible drunken sex, expensive jewelry found on sidewalks, blank checks, renewed friendships, and America's rise on the list of beer consumption per capita.

AMERICAN PIE

Sex Toys: Everyone knows the “apple pie” scene from this movie, but have you seen the deleted “beer bottle” scenes? I thought not. Picture this: beer bottles as dildos. I know, little crazy—but think about it: the top of the bottle is ribbed for her pleasure and the upper half is skinny so it’ll warm her up for the larger bottom half. They can’t get whiskey dick, and they last as long as you want! Is this creeping you out or what?! High five!

The Crew: All right, . . . you’ll need a loser, a nerd, a jock, a party animal, and four girls whose combined IQ is six.

Ingredients: Booze, bitches, and bros!

Beer! Fuck, Yeah! Beer! Fuck yeah!

Objective: To get laid. Duh.

How to Get Totally Faded, Bro!

- Each time Jim’s dad talks, drink one. This is just hilarious as is.
- Each time Stifler says, “To engage in intercourse,” in an awesomely Stifler way, drink three.
- Each time Stifler’s mom is mentioned (including “MILF!”), drink two and listen as the inevitable story comes up between your friends about, “That one guy in high school who boned that mom . . .”
- Each time a college is mentioned, drink one. If it happens to be your college, you still drink one. You aren’t special.
- Each time someone is holding alcohol, drink one and proceed to throw a massive party where hundreds of people, liquor,

and loud music appear out of nowhere. If possible, swing from the chandelier.

- Each time someone gives a supposedly motivational speech that in real life would be really fucking stupid, drink two.
- When someone gets laid: finish your drink, cheer for his success, think back to your awkward first time, and finish your neighbor's drink to wash away the memory.

Sex Toys: No, but really: beer bottles as dildos. It's fucking genius. You can get eighteen for, like, twelve bucks. It's a bargain. Get on it.

SUPER TROOPERS

Driving Under the Influence (DUI): This is a very serious topic and not one to joke about, unless of course the joke contained the punch line, "Chomping on my chode," which is just too funny to pass up. The joke could also be a fart joke; I think we can all agree on that. I guess what I'm saying is that chomping on a farting chode is funnier than a DUI. Whew, glad I got that out of my system.

Cadets: If you have a pulse, you will laugh during this movie.

Supplies:
- Disregard for the law . . . or proper internal health
- Handcuffs (seriously)

Booze! Hey, when you're a cop, there's no one to give you a DUI! Ha ha, fuckers!

Objective: To mess with Farva

How to Drink like a Vermont state trooper:

- Each time a cop does something illegal, drink two and tell everyone about the second time you got crabs.
- Whenever someone calls Rabbit "Rookie," drink two and light someone's country music award on fire.
- When a siren turns on, drink one and "Say car, ramrod."
- Each time Farva gets something sprayed or thrown or spilled on him, drink two and bear-bearfucker, do you need assistance?
- Whenever someone says "Ramathorn" or "Farva," drink one and sing it again, rookie bitch!
- Waterfall during the entire syrup-chugging scene until the snozzberries taste like snozzberries. Important: If anyone doesn't waterfall through the whole thing, he gets to wear the handcuffs mentioned under Supplies for the rest of the movie. Seriously. Way funny.

Drinking Under the Influence (the *Other* DUI): A very serious issue facing today's young drinkers is drinking under the influence. See, when you drink while sober, you can pace yourself based where you plan on going or what you plan on doing. But when you're drunk, not only can you take double shots of Patron with no chaser, but you also don't notice how drunk you're getting, and all of a sudden you're fucked-out-of-your-mind drunk!

Oh, did I say this was a problem? My bad. Small typo. I meant to say drinking under the influence is "the epitome of greatness and represents the perfection of God's creation." You see how I could mix those up.

OLD SCHOOL

Growing Up: It's like drinking games—you start out with the simple life: Flip Cup, Quarters, Baseball. And then you hit puberty and start experiencing new things, such as playing with girls in games like Power Hour and Three Man. Before you know it, you're all grown up, playing complex games like Beer Die and Assault Quarters, but always long for the simplicities of youth in games like Thumper! and Horse Races.

Players: I think playing with gang members could be fun, but regular people will work, too.

Supplies:
- Beer bong
- Snoop Dogg

Beer: Enough to drown a fish

Objective: Do whatever it takes to find yourself Jell-O wrestling two topless coeds . . . what did I just write? I blacked out.

Drink-a-Palooza
- Each time you can directly relate to something happening in the movie, quietly drink two and think about whether you should mention it or not.
- Each time Vince Vaughn disgraces the idea of marriage verbally or physically, drink two, rewind it, and play it again. Some of the best advice you'll ever hear.
- Each time someone says, "Godfather," drink one. Next time you go out, choose someone to be the Godfather. Call him this at opportune moments. Never tell anyone why. Drink

one for each female who wants to "get to know" the Godfather.

- When someone says, "Blue," drink one. If they say, "Magenta," finish your drink.
- If you can name ten fraternities and ten sororities, drink five. Fuck you; it's relevant.
- Each time the pledges are forced to do something, force yourself to drink one. I know: hazing can be rough sometimes.
- Each time someone watching the movie asks, "What other movies is Dean Pritchard in?" drink four and smack him for disgracing Jeremy Piven.
- Each time you hear a line that you've heard someone quote a hundred times over the last five years, drink three and fill it up again!

Haze-a-Palooza: If you're in a fraternity and someone playing is a pledge, he abides by all the above rules as well as the following:

- Each time someone else drinks, he drinks. And yes, if there's a scene with ten people drinking, then it's ten drinks, pledge.
- Each time Mitch doesn't want to do something or is hesitant, drink two. You won't be so hesitant after the fourteenth beer. Now go lose your V-card.

What Your Major Really Means

Saying: I'm studying to become an anthropologist.
Translation: If that falls through I'll be a chimney sweep, or some other profession that doesn't exist.
Saying: I'm studying Poli Sci.
Translation: God should have made me a mute.
Saying: I'm studying jazz piano.
Translation: Stop. Stop laughing at me. It's my passion. Fuck you guys!

Saying: I'm studying geography.
Translation: Because there is no "real estate" major.
Saying: I'm a communication major.
Translation: I've been drunk for four straight years.
Saying: I'm studying economics.
Translation: I got rejected from the finance program.

EUROTRIP

Europe Sucks: Every twenty-two- to thirty-year-old American wants to go backpacking through Europe so he can experience the joy of being a destitute nomad who's hated by everyone. He gets to spend his life's savings on food from sections in Safeway he usually walks past very quickly, eat the saliva of various French waiters, and experience being lost for long periods of time.

How to Make Europe Rock: Go to Amsterdam. Bang a Scandinavian. Drink Guinness.

Players: So, like, what ethnicity are Swiss people?

Supplies:

- A list of affordable youth hostels
- Warmed-up knuckles to fend off creepers who are staying at affordable youth hostels
- A list of Americanized hotels that serve Budweiser

Beer: What we know as "imported"

Objective: To return home, claim to be cultured, and bang a naive American

"Come on, Baby, It's How Europeans Do It . . ."

- Every time there is a European stereotype, an angel gets its wings. Also, drink two.
- For each individual boob shown, drink one. Girl *and* guy.
- Each time they go to a new country, drink two and make a lame joke insulting that country. Last one to make a joke drinks an additional three.
- Every time a player says something about a time he went to Europe that doesn't begin with either, "So I'm hammered in Amsterdam . . ." or "So I'm balls deep in this French chick on top of the Arc de Triomphe . . . ," he drinks five. No one cares.
- Each time Jenny is not considered a female object of desire, drink two and have a chauvinistic discussion about whether she's hot/how many beers it'd take to make her hot.
- Each time you wish you could be one of the Manchester United fans, drink one. During the "*French bastards! Get on the other side of the road, you pricks! Go on out of it! Fuck off!*" scene, mute the TV and create your own whole new level of cussing.
- Whenever Scotty doesn't know, drink one. And yes, we know it's Matt Damon.

If Anybody Playing Is from Europe: Obviously they can drink all us pussy Americans under the table. Therefore, they get to drink eight drinks every time Mieke is mentioned.

ROAD TRIP

Don't even try to say you haven't thought about ways to kill people with alcohol. The first idea is always the cocktail umbrella to the neck, right? The problem is that it's obvious to others. I prefer slipping on a well-placed ice cube and catching myself by plunging the umbrella into his jugular vein—problem solved! There's also the injection of straight Everclear, shards of glass hidden in Guinness, or the all-time classic: Flaming Dr. Pepper-to-the-eyes combo. What's your favorite?!

Note to Mom: I'm kidding. Chill.

Players: People who aren't afraid to have fun at a stranger's expense

Supplies:
- A really shitty car
- Even shittier beer (mixing in dirt isn't out of the question)
- The ability to get lost and wind up somewhere that should totally suck but turns out to be an eye-opening, intoxicating experience

Objective: To lower America's ranking in no less than three internationally respected categories

Getting There:
- Each time someone drinks, drink one. Each time someone takes a hit, call your supplier.
- Each time Barry (Tom Green) narrates the story, drink one. Each time you Google the University of Ithaca to see how to apply, stop drinking to conserve the few brain cells you have left.

- When the fury is being urged to unleash itself, drink three. When the fury is unleashed, finish your drink.
- Drink one for each nipple you would happily lick.
- Each time Sean William Scott does the exact same character he did from *American Pie* (Stifler), drink one.
- Whenever a scene reminds you of something you've done, drink two. If it involves boobs, drink three. If it involves inventing untraceable marijuana, you are awesome.

If You Are from Boston or Austin: You get to hand out three drinks each time your city is mentioned. Also, if you could please explain why there are so many fucking songs about Austin and Boston, it'd be great. Thanks.

VAN WILDER

Postcollege binge drinking is considered alcoholism. This is why you must learn to "network." Networking is drinking at a bar while wearing a suit and swapping business cards with people who apparently don't recycle enough already. With phrases like, "discussed the merger over drinks" and "consulted on the Wilson file," you'll be justifying your alcoholism in no time! And never forget—you can always go back to college to do a PhD: Plenty of Hard Drinking!

Players: Underagers, college students, and networkers

Supplies: Fake ID, keg tap, pin-striped suit

Beer: Busch Light, Miller High Life, Hefeweizen

"Drink Beer" . . . that's "Reeb Knird" Backward:

- Every time Van says, "Write that down," replace "write" with "drink" and "that down" with "two." Just making it simpler for you.
- Each timer Richard says something medical, drink one. Drink two if it's used as an insult. Drink three if you know what the medical term means. Drink four if you can spell it. Drink five if you just drank four.
- Each time Taj says, "Have sex," in some great metaphorical way, drink three and tell your boys about the time you "dined at the pink taco stand."
- Each time an elementary school kid drinks or pukes, drink two and comment on how deprived your childhood was.
- Kissing, drink one. Sex, drink four. Defecating into a garbage can, drink six.
- Whenever Van is riding in his golf cart, drink two and have the same conversation you've had eight million times about how cool it'd be to have your own golf cart.

High School Drinking: Have older brother buy Busch Light and Mike's Hard Lemonade, drink heavily and shotgun messily, be too nervous to hook up with girls. Sometimes puke.

College Drinking: Have upperclassmen buy case upon case of whatever is on sale. Pound flavored vodka with no chaser and beer bong three beers at a time. Hook up with so many girls your dick becomes tired. Kick yourself for not hooking up as much in high school.

Postcollege Drinking: Go to bars that are classy according to random blogs you found on Google. Order gin and tonics. Say lines to women you've been picturing in your head since you were seventeen. Wonder if you should take off your suit jacket or not.

SPECIAL THANKS GOES TO . . .

Livers everywhere, the ability to justify drinking six nights a week while working and in school, loose morals, that giant beer bong from the balcony to the front lawn, the inventor of keg cups, peeing off of high places, liquid confidence, the invention of keyboards because my handwriting blows ass, roman candle fights, ibuprofen, the wonderful hangover-curing people at Gatorade, IHOP, three A.M. Taco Bell runs, the twins at Muchas Gracias, friends with discounts who work at restaurants so I can afford to eat real food, entirely too low-cut tank tops and their interior contents, Pike vs. Gamma Phi Beta flip cup battles, the P.B.D.L., caffeine, not having class Friday, whoever decided Communication Studies was a legitimate major (seriously?), open bars, biads, triads, outrageously massive Halloween parties, Beer Olympics, date functions, giant speakers that drown out the hassle of carrying on a conversation, Kings and its ability to get girls drunk, Pi Kappa Alpha, Palm Tree (Ha!), God for having a sense of humor, cops who I can run faster than, pizza fights, Greeks vs. Tekes snowball fights, Canada's not having any rules, brotherhoods, Edward 40 Hands, digital cameras to capture the shit-show that is my life, literary people who can drink me under the table, offensive comments, sober people who drive us places, ridiculous tax reductions because I used beer for researching this book, weekend brunch at sororities, whoever came up with the 30-bomb, Oregon for having no tax and cheap liquor, my mom for giving me the idea for this book in a drunkenly roundabout way, my mom for editing this whole book, my mom for making me martinis whenever I'm sick, bench presses and dumbbells everywhere, road trips, Vegas, Mexico, SparkNotes, scantrons and professors who only use one version of an exam, summer and its ability to remove girls' clothes, seriously meaningful moments that make you realize you should do what you love and not what everyone says you should do, hot girlfriends who bring over hot friends, girls that drink beer with the boys, knowing the campus police's daughters, disregarding social norms, Duncan's trombone that wakes me up for Husky games, Husky games, my agent Scott Hoffman, my acquisition editor, Jason Pinter, for being exactly like me but six years older, my new editor, Marc Resnick, for embracing *The Imbible* with open arms and a willing liver, Kylah McNeil and Sarah Lumnah for being the coolest publishing assistants ever, big comfortable chairs and being able to disregard their various stains, cheesy but profitable marketing ploys, pelting cars with water balloons, drunken barbecues, stealing couches, drunken sing-alongs, impromptu dance parties, acorn fights while locked on the balcony, pranks, whipped cream and all its various uses, balcony-testing things that shouldn't be balcony-tested, boobs, the Rush Quad, ex-bosses who drove me to never work a job that I didn't love even if it paid well, Mr. Carlo Rossi, sexual-innuendo-themed parties, the Whistler or Bust Crew, the metaphor that is going balls deep, the nonmetaphor that is going balls deep, QFC Advantage Card Discounts on beer, microwaves to cook me cheap meals until my writing advance came through, cheap meals, writing advances, Barry Jones for finally fixing the Internet connection so I can get e-mails from my agent, my dad for always supporting me and paying for college so I had more time to do research for this book, my twin brother for actually approving of my authorship (this is rare for twins), my sister and Grace for playing board games with me when I get home hammered at three A.M., The Ram's one-pound extreme husky burger, student discounts, Safeway Club Card discounts, hand sanitizer to save me from infecting my keyboard, my creative writing teacher who told me to write something funny so the class would stop being so fucking depressing and introspective, flasks, protein powder and its ability to make me large and scare people I don't want to fight, penny slots and free drinks, air-conditioning and its ability to destroy back sauce, the Couve, friends who looked exactly like their older brothers when we were in high school so they could buy us beer, Mike Rupp for giving me funny suggestions for random parts of this book, Ross's contagious laugh, J-Talb's phone voice, TwoHole for making me drink on the few nights I decide to take off, Slop for being the ultimate drinking buddy and helping me justify drinking the night before an exam, Lance for feeding me entirely too-expensive liquor, Pcam for getting us all drunk at work, DevCakes—my Lids partner—for doing all the drunken shit that I was too afraid to try, the Commissioner of the P.B.D.L., Big Big and the Snakesssss, my awesome girlfriend who always supports my getting way too drunk all the time and laughs at my stupid outrageous comments, Shane for being entirely too tall, Pap for providing me with nonstop unintentional hilarity, Big Il for having poor international currency, Lance for making me feel so weak I just gave up and started writing, JV for making me feel so strong I started again, Whitey for drunken front-porch sing-alongs, Alpha Gamma Delta for applauding our drunken sing-alongs, Landon for playing my drunk ass to sleep with classical guitar, everyone else that put up with me getting way too drunk all the time and laughing at my stupid outrageous comments, Willow for being our test dummy, Party Ian for always knowing where the party is at, Crispin Thurlow for being the coolest professor ever and putting up with me coming to class hammered, Jamie Moshin and our discussion of the chode, Jeff Ridenour for helping me say "banged her with a cigar" in Spanish, Aaron the weather TA for looking past Slop and my "interesting-smelling" nalgenes, Bash & TheOrangutan's Wild 'n' Crazy Adventures, Slut Bag for showing me the ways of the slut, G-Dub for putting up with my obviously drunken sales presentations, generational gaps that hide my obviously drunken sales presentations, Bob Barker in general, Dave Barry for being the funniest person to ever live, Tucker Max, Maddox and the College Humor crew for writing funny shit to jog my brain during writer's block, my awesome research partner (Google), my helpful assistant (Wikipedia), my mind refocuser (general Internet porn), the human body and its ability to function on three hours of sleep a night and four pints of vodka a day during Whistler College Invasion, meeting random people in random places and going on random adventures, tinted computer screens, Visine, general mooning and showing of the butt, Rockstar, Monster, Amped, Wired, Red Bull, quadruple-shot espressos, Man-Law, trivia night, the Mug Club, Altoids to conceal my rum-breath, Frank Kelley Rich for popularizing literary alcoholism, extreme alcoholics who take the focus away from my only moderately extreme drinking habits, stupid people who make me look smart, friends who let me use their old essays for classes I'm taking, big schools that never look too much into each student's attendance vs. grade record, summer lock-ins, Alex from Vermont and our undefeated summer of Beer Pong and passing out under couches, the Bud Light float on the Yakima River, Meredith Hays for giving me guidance, Bob Diforio and Peter Lynch for giving me a chance, Pink Floyd laser light shows, rock-out jam sessions in the basement with Marky Mark, Greek Week, Car Jams, foam parties, entirely too-strong screwdrivers for breakfast, seaside weekends, writing on the job, knowing bartenders and bouncers, cop radars in my friend's fast cars, bunk beds and their many hidden uses, stealing composites, doubling down, doing things on Husky Stadium's fifty-yard line that were not meant to be done there, birthday shots, twenty-one runs, the annual Bash Bash, and everybody and everything else that has gone in to making my life what it is today: completely fucking awesome.

Always Remember . . .

It's not whether you win or lose . . . it's how drunk you get while playing the game.

—Homer Simpson